A Guru in the Guest Room

"Books on enlightenment don't always get this real in order to show you the unreal. It ends with the deepest wisdom of all, wrapped up in such plain English that you may not know what hit you."

Scott Kiloby, author of *Living Realization* and *The Natural Rest Method*

"One of the characters in this book is one of the greatest fictional Gurus in history. I'm just not saying which one."

Jerry Katz, Nonduality.com, Editor: *One-Essential Writings On Nonduality*

"Swami Z is more real than the so-called real swamis. A delightful read steeped in common sense wisdom with a twist of laughter."

John Troy, author of *Wisdom's Soft Whisper*

"Vicki Woodyard is The Queen of Non-do-ality!"

Tony Cartledge, author of *Planetary Types: the Science of Celestial Influence*

"Swami Z's late-in-the-alphabet name hints that this constructed image can be the last such image a reader would need. His various roles in the book invite you to stand up tall and step forward."

Greg Goode, author of *Standing As Awareness, Direct Path: A User Guide*, and *Emptiness and Joyful Freedom*

" If you like your spirituality served up with wisdom, cookies and lots of love, then here's your dish."

Chuck Hillig, author of *Enlightenment for Beginners*, *Seeds for the Soul*, *The Way IT Is*, *Looking for God: Seeing the Whole in One*, and *The Magic King*

"If you're in the mood for spiritual wisdom marinated in divine comedy—treat yourself!"

Elsa Bailey, Concord, CA

A Guru in the Guest Room

Vicki Woodyard

For friends and lovers of truth, who sometimes forget that they, too, are The Self. What else can you be?

ACKNOWLEDGEMENTS

This book has been brewing for over ten years. A huge plate of cookies to all of Swami's original devotees, who laughed and cried with me while he was being born. Myra, Sam, Aly, Michael, Kathy, Gloria, and all of the satsang gang.

To Jerry Katz, of Nonduality.com., a friend and the original Nondual Guy.

To Chris O'Byrne, my editor and publisher at Red Willow Publishing, who cleaned up after me, sweeping away the extra ellipses, em dashes and stuff.

To Rob, for making room in the house for a little Swami to live.

To Swami himself, who as a piece of fiction, is one of the realest people I have ever not met.

To Monica and Connie and Betty for keeping me aligned with my purpose.

For Laurie, Bob, Peter and John, who have gone on but are ever-present.

And last but not least, to my dear online readers who have allowed me to share heart space with them across the Internet and beyond. Namaste.

Table of Contents

FOREWORD..xvii
PROLOGUE...xix

PART I

Prasad from a Pez Dispenser...2
Swami Z, An Incarnation of Love..4
Alone..5
Holding the Bag 6
Initiation...7
A Boat to the Other Shore...8
Swami's Hammock 9
Nothing to Do 10
My Creation 12
Pop Goes The Weasel..13
Reality...15
Autumn 16
Halloween 17
The Teacher is Always with You......................................19
War...21
Just a Device 22
Naptime...24
More Than Anything..25
Attracted to Shiny Objects 27
At Swami's Table 28
Making Sense of Christmas 29
The Journey Without Distance...30
Christmas Eve with Swami..32
The Flimsiest Day of the Year...34
What Do You Want Me To Do? 35
Smelling Like Vanilla..37
A New Year 38
Be What You Are 39

The Ankles of a Swami 41
Soliloquy 42
Yoga with Swami Z..44
Karmic Seeds 45
Valentine's with Swami...46
Are You Having a Fresh Experience? 48
Then Comes the Silence..49
The Wings of a Swami 50
All I Saw Was Everything......................................51
Unreal...52
Orphan..54
Stuck 55

PART II

The Nuances of Home 58
The Question..60
Satsang with Swami Z 61
Surrender to the Impossible 63
The First Visitor 65
Everything Means Everything 66
All or Nothing 68
The Curmudgeon 69
Vicki's Satsang..71
Getting Down to Business 73
Bliss of the Self..74
The Bic Guru..76
Breakdown 77
Nothing Ever Changes 79
The Sixty-Four Dollar Question 81
Heartthrob 83
The Guru Walk of Fame..85
Gone Hollywood 87
Prayerful...88
Opening the Door...90
Swami's Grace 91

The Truth is Neither Here Nor There 92
Slice and Bake Enlightenment 94
It's Not About the Cookies 96
The Price of Admission 97
Saturday Night 98
The Game 99
Initiation into Now 100
Nuisance 102
Above the Opposites 103
Stick Pony Drill 104
A Rhetorical Question 105
"Satsnag" 106
It's in the Script 107
Where We Are Joined to God 108
Priceless 109
Snit 110
A Gold Mine 111
A Giggle 113
The Essence of the Teachings 114
Swami's Kindness 115
More in Love 116
Witnessing the Chaos 118
The Law of Levity 119
Gurus Are Out 120
On Having No Head 122

PART III

The True Guru 126
Larry and Ruin 127
Stick Pony Wisdom—Learning to Ride Like the Wind 128
Wind Horse 130
Two Left Feet 132
Through "Think and Then" 133
An Appetite for Satsang 135
Inside Out and Upside Down 136

Frustration 138
Just a Piece of Fiction 139
Hunger.. 141
Larry's Turn 143
Sea Change.. 145
Summer with Swami Z 147
Riding for a Fall.. 149
Sitting Ducks... 151
Through the Eye of the Needle 153
The Art of Being Nothing 154
So Much Love.. 156
A Cocoa Mustache 158
At My Worst... 159
Eden 161
Green with Envy 162
A Turn for the Worse.. 163
In a Rut... 166
A Measly Excuse.. 167
Snit City 168
Quickening... 170
Not Fade Away.. 172
Nirvana... 173
Spiritual Honesty 175
A Disciple of a Concept 177
When There is Nothing Left to Do, Do It!....................... 180
A Question 181
On the Brink.. 183
Food Fight.. 185
Biting The Big Twinkie.. 186
And So to Bed.. 187
The Last Waltz 189

ABOUT THE AUTHOR.. 191

FOREWORD

For centuries, luminous minds have known that humor is a powerful factor in human healing, whether the suffering is physical, mental, psychic or spiritual. "Laughter is the sun that drives winter from the human face," observed our friend Victor Hugo.

Luckily for us, our wondrous Vicki Woodyard knows the divine quality of humor, too—having learned it firsthand from within. As some of you already know, Vicki has travelled through grief, loss and profound angst many times in her life journey. And the fact that she has come up from these depths with the Swami Z's Awakened Wink is a miracle. In this second book, *A Guru in the Guest Room*, Vicki shares her Awakened Wink miracle with all of us.

If you're in the mood for spiritual wisdom marinated in divine comedy—treat yourself!

Elsa Bailey, Concord, CA

PROLOGUE

"Swami told me that he had to reach through my broken heart to teach people anything at all. He didn't tell me that I would be laughing through my tears as I wrote him."

Vicki Woodyard

Swami Z is an iMac-ulate conception born during one of the hardest times of my life. My husband was dying of cancer and I had begun a website to support him. When he asked me to find my passion before he died, little did I know that it would be to become a spiritual writer.

Writing offered me relief from the sometimes unrelenting grief. One day I saw something called The Awakened Teachers List online. It seemed very presumptuous to actually make a list like that. I wrote a sendup of it and called it The Sleeping Teachers List. Swami Z grew out of that.

I called him Swami Z because he snored. He began as a cartoonish character that wore a bed sheet and hung around the Sleep Department at Macy's. He carried a large Sharpie pen to autograph people's sheets. But soon Macy's wasn't big enough to hold him; so he came to live with me. His kitchen table wisdom soon became popular because of its unfettered honesty.

His character was very opposite to me, whom I portray in the book as "hapless and feckless." But I have full freedom to create a guru that is an endearing if pesky little rascal. Wisdom is born from the opposites. I let thunder and lightning strike the two of them as they dance through the essays learning and teaching as they go.

The essays were written over a period of ten years, so there is more than one Christmas celebration, etc., as Swami and Vicki

roll through the days of their lives. Part I begins with Swami first coming to live with Vicki. In Part II, she builds a room onto her house just so that Swami can hold satsang. In Part III, things continue to unfold.

It is my joy to write his character. Over time I learned that he is the Self and a teacher of the heart. More than that, I cannot say. So let's get on with it....

PART I

"Sometimes I feel that Swami Z can read my mind—that he is peeping into my deeps and seeing—nothing."

Vicki Woodyard

Prasad from a Pez Dispenser

I met Swami Z today in the Sleep Department at Macy's and I am in love. After taking many incarnations (and often subways) to achieve enlightenment, I now find a man who is giving it away for free. And his kindness is such that if you don't like it, he will also take it back. I tell you, I was taken aback. There is nothing that this Swami of the Jammies will not do. He allows anyone to attend satsang. And I mean anyone—even if they are wearing robes and calling themselves silly names. You can bring your blanket and suck your thumb. You can suck his thumb; he doesn't care.

I had one question that I wanted Swami Z to answer. Would I be getting enlightened this lifetime? Of course I would, I was told. As soon as he took his groupies to lunch. I'm sorry—what he really said was, "You groupies are out to lunch!"

What I totally love about Swami Z is his ability to dispense junk food while remaining blissfully unaware of the calories. No other guru knows so little about what is good for you. His magnanimity is matched only by his paunch. I am quite paunch-drunk, in love, bowled over by this guru giving satsang while counting his sheep. Some gurus would shear them, but not Swami Z.

He asked me what I wanted for Christmas and when I told him that I wanted all the children of the world to be fed one decent meal, he offered to make it for them. Sad, but true. His cookie habit would sicken more than it would heal. I tried to question him about his life pre-enlightenment, but he said that like everything else in his life, it was a snore. I wanted more. He thought I said "Smores," because he has those, too.

I said, "Can you tell me what life as a child was like for you?"

"Of course," he said, rummaging through his box of Cocoa Puffs with a misty eye. "Of course I can, but I won't." And that pretty much sums up the teaching.

Swami Z, An Incarnation of Love

My love for Swami Z increases hourly. When I asked him how it was that he came to be an incarnation of love, he said that he wasn't until you added two parts water. That opened my tear ducts right up. Pretty soon I was sniffling through my ears. Perfect. Perhaps now I could make sense out of something that the sleeping swami had to say. Because love of this sort must make sense—mustn't it? As I dried my ears and blew my nose and wiped off the front of my shirt, he sat blissfully opposite from me, fiddling with his Pez dispenser. I knew that prasad could not be far behind. "Swami, Oh Great Sleeping One, how is it that you have created this love and placed it in my heart—and a Pez in my hand—how can this be done? Can love be created?" I said in awe and wonder.

Swami Z often saws logs of deep insight and makes a great dharma fire. Those who seek his wisdom gather 'round his warmth and bask in his glow—if he has remembered to use his deodorant that day. But that's another story. It's been said that the Great Ones never emit bodily odors of the unpleasant kind, but that is not always true. Actually Swami smells like a baby that has just spit up, especially if he has let the milk sour on his Cocoa Puffs. It's just slightly revolting and pretty endearing. One of his wisdom logs says this: When you sleep, sleep fully. Do not sleep with waking mind. And if you do, enjoy it anyway. Once he slept so fully that he communicated the Living Wisdom to an entire county and three tree frogs.

Bliss is just another word for forgetting what you know. Knowledge too often applied is worse than too much butter on a baked potato—can't get too much. Enjoy. The Swami's words ring true, but his snore roars.

Alone

Swami Z and I sat in the kitchen. "I am all alone," he said. "Do you know that you, too, are all alone in this big, big world?" Surprised, I studied his face. The light was dim and I could see his wrinkles. Usually, I didn't notice. But tonight I just sat and took him in.

"No one really knows me," said Swami Z, stirring his cereal calmly. "Do you know that you, too, are all alone on this cruel planet?" I couldn't think of a word to say that would comfort him. I just watched his weariness as it slowly spread across the messy old kitchen. "Sometimes," he said pensively, "sometimes this truth, too, has its place." I never did manage to say anything. For the longest time we just sat together eating our cold cereal.

Holding the Bag

"Swami," I said, in a fit of pique, "why don't you move along—don't you have someone else to mystify besides me?"

"Oh, you're the only game in town for me," he said with a goofy little grin. "Besides," he said as he ate his fifth cookie of the morning, "if you looked inside your own mind, I wouldn't have to do it. Just look, and like the wind, it's gone. Thoughts would disappear and so would you."

"Right—like those cookies I just opened." His little tummy was bulging with cookies and I was left holding the bag—Pecan Sandies, my favorite.

Initiation

Today is my birthday and Swami Z has promised to give me a new name. I am wearing orange, if that's a clue. "Close your eyes," said Swami as he spun me around three times. I felt a cool pressure around the area of my third eye. Had I been accepted as a sannyasin?

Eagerly, I jumped to my usual conclusions, hitting my knee on a kitchen chair. I hobbled over to Swami, and he gave me a bear hug and pointed to the mirror hanging in the dining room. I eagerly hopped in there to take a look, anticipating a tilak on my forehead at least.

I went right to the mirror and I don't think Swami will mind me sharing this. I am now Navel Sunkist #3107. I have arrived. I am nobody!

A Boat to the Other Shore

Swami is like a boat to the other shore—if you get my drift. He does the duality dog paddle extremely well for an old man. I long for him while I am in his presence. I think it's because he never gives me the satisfaction of letting me love him as I want to do. And I want him to reciprocate. I want a fair trade. I march along with him, jump into the pond with him, longing for him to look directly at me and say, "There you are! I love you and I will never leave you."

When he says it, I will let you know. It would be comparable to—I don't know if there is a comparable.

But so far, he just hangs out with me, instructing me on how to slice the cookies more evenly or begging me to give him more raw dough than any old man should eat. I know that he is lovable—but is he faithful? After all, he tends to vanish like his plates of warm cookies. A hint of vanilla hanging in the air is all that's left. Yesterday he walked by the elementary school and joined in recess. In a rope swing, his old legs were pumping and soon all the kids were following him. I would like to be one of those kids following Swami. But often he is inscrutable and unsuitable. Just a dumb old doughboy.

Swami's Hammock

"Rest and rapture. What else is there?"

Pamela Wilson

Last summer I spent some time in Swami's hammock. Cocooned in remnants of cookie dough, we would laze the afternoon away. Now that winter is approaching, we will still have our quiet times—because basically that is who Swami is. He is just an old man in a blissed-out state. "Resting from your mind should be a regular occupation," said Swami from his chair at the kitchen table. He had sat down after mopping up the floor when some of his cookie dough stuck to it.

"I don't know how to rest my mind. It just swamps me so quickly." I rolled my eyes in mock peril. To my surprise his sleepy old eyes threw sparks at me.

"Don't you know what a bother you are to yourself? Never mind me," he said. "Never mind anyone else. You drive yourself nuts and it's all I can do to keep my own composure."

"Don't you think my mind gives me enough trouble without yours adding to the mix?" he added.

"But, Swami...."

"Don't you 'but, Swami' me. I've had quite enough of you and your mind. Keep it to yourself."

Oddly enough, the minute I took it back consciously, it disappeared. I was back in Swami's hammock.

Nothing to Do

"Live with skillful nonchalance and ceaseless concern."
Prajnaparamita Sutra

There is nowhere to go and nothing to do. But only after a serious incarnation's worth of "going and doing" do we know that. Let's face it. All of us have eagerly read the books about being one with everything, knowing yourself as the Self, chopping wood and carrying water, mountains becoming mountains, et cetera. I never did get it until Swami got a hold of me. He gave it to me by osmosis, which is not to be confused with halitosis. His cookie breath is ambrosial. He is so long in the tooth that he is tripping over it—but I digreth, I mean *digress*. "I guess" is one of Swami Z's expressions that drives me to blink.

Here is a sample of one of our recent conversations:

"Swami, are you enlightened?"

"I guess."

"You mean that a person could be enlightened and not even know that he was?"

"I guess."

"Can you give me enlightenment, Swami?"

"I guess."

"You are driving me nuts, bonkers. Can't you do better than guess?"

"You are not even close to getting there and I don't want to hurt your feelings," was his reply.

"Have you heard the story about the bird who flew over the mountaintops with a scarf in his mouth? As long as it takes to wear the mountains down, that is how long it takes one to achieve enlightenment," said Swami.

"So you can't give it to me, can you? Admit it! You are going senile on me—you old—you—you...."

You guessed it. Swami had fallen asleep while looking for my original face.

Oh, well, tomorrow is another illusion.

My Creation

Sad to say, Swami has stopped looking for his original face and is, instead, looking for his glasses, which are on top of his head, along with a layer of lint. Why the lint? Because some words are funnier than others—and since Swami only exists because he is my creation, I can make him wear a feather boa or worse. If he knows what is good for him, he will stop feeding me all the straight lines and give me some of the good ones.

Speaking of lines, the Swami is becoming increasingly famous at Macy's. Nothing that I can do will persuade him that people in the Sleep Department are not in more need of awakening than others. I fear that he will fall down the Up escalator and hurt himself. He is a little long in the tooth and he keeps tripping over it. Dental karma is the worst.

Sometimes he stands by the cash register and goes *ka-ching* over and over. When I ask him to stop, he throws a teaching tantrum, throwing himself on the floor screaming, "I want my mantra. I want my mantra!" If his mantra materializes, I will let you know. Those of us who love him are growing impatient for their enlightenment moment. But it seems that all he has are "senior" ones. You gotta love him—or else. Who else can I write about that lights up the room the way that he does?

What does this have to do with enlightenment? I wonder myself. After he goes to bed, I snatch the remote and try to retrace his steps. All the great ones leave footprints. Swami leaves right after the weather forecast. His followers always know if it will rain if they but listen.

Side note: I just want to let everyone know that Swami Z will be happy to help you look for your original face. He is willing to go so far as to accompany you to the plastic surgeon's office. He will not stay for the surgery, however, as he is squeamish.

Pop Goes The Weasel

"Mmph...ppphhm...oommph...." Swami sat bolt upright in his kitchen chair, the chords in his neck sticking out. He continued, "mmmph...."

"Swami, what in the heck are you doing?" I said. "You look like you're about to pop a blood vessel."

He looked at me while continuing to utter oddities like "moommph!"

He shook his head sadly, saying, "No good, no good." He stood up dizzily from his kitchen chair. At one point he almost tipped over. He was just about to fall back when I caught him by the shoulders and gently set him right. He looked down at his gently rising paunch and patted it as if he were a new-born babe.

"What is it that was causing you so much distress, Swami?"

"I was trying to force a thought into my mind, but it got away. Maybe if I had tried just a little harder." His even-now purplish face told me that it was a good idea that he had stopped.

"What was the thought about? What were you wanting to think, but just couldn't?" I had bitten, much like I did when he pulled a sheet of cookies from the oven.

"I don't know—I can't tell you—because I couldn't get the thought to come into my mind. And there are other thoughts that I can't get out." He looked pitifully present in his admitted ignorance.

We sat there together in silence. Suddenly, Swami sang out, "Pop goes the weasel!"

I replied as best I could. "Bye, bye, Miss American Pie...." We were letting go of songs that had been running through our respective minds. That's all. Whatever. At least I knew that Swami was human, God bless him. Otherwise, he wouldn't be able to stay here on earth with me. Thank heaven for small favors.

Reality

It's not always rosy between the two of us. Between you and me, he's just a lonely old man needing love. If you can find it in your heart to let him know that he is, as Stuart Smalley would say, okay just as he is, I will see that he gets the message. Lord knows, I am getting his. The man has issues. I can see us now on Dr. Phil. He could devote one twenty-minute segment just to us and our warped relationship. It is a love-hate one, disguised as guru and disciple. Underneath, he is a mass of seething hostilities. Dr. Phil has chairs that he puts his guests in. When he has brought them to a fever pitch of confession, he suddenly turns the warring guests to face each other.

"So, Swami," I hear Dr. Phil saying, "what is it about Vicki that irritates you so much?"

"Oh, she is loving me to death. I need my space, I need to be able to go into my room and scratch myself—and she's always following me around begging for enlightenment."

"How's that working for you, Vicki?" asks Dr. Phil.

I grumble under my breath that it's working about as well as this bit. Swami has gotten me up at 2:00 a.m. to write this and I am beyond cross. Forget the great beyond, the boat to the other shore; I want to get some rest from this iMac-ulate delusion.

"And you, Swami Z, how do you feel about your creator-disciple cum cookie-maker, Vicki?" asks the good doctor.

"Never saw her before in my life," he sez.

We will be appearing next on People's Court and I will be suing him for all he's worth—for what it's worth.

Autumn

The leaves are falling from the trees as we sit in the backyard. Watching the squirrels fly across the yard, we mirror each other's contentment. "See that one over there?" Swami said, pointing to a young squirrel scampering up a nearby tree. "Sometimes you are just as squirrelly. I watch your mind trying to save wisdom for the winter. Making notes of what I say and in what context I said it." The little old man had me there. I have a notebook filled with Swami's wisdoms. (Not his teeth, but his sayings, which have teeth.) Are you getting confused? Swami hopes so. At one time I had thought of turning him into a book, but he refuses to be Flavor of the Month for anyone. He sees success coming and runs the other way. Frequently he hits his head, I admit; but his dottiness only adds to his charm.

"Nothing worse than being trapped by a would-be disciple," is one of his wisdoms. "Nothing better than catching one and releasing it back into the wild, once again able to care for himself."

To that end, he keeps traps ready and waiting. If he ever asks you to tell him if a dog has buddha nature, watch out. He may be distracting you to trap you into a king-sized box of Cocoa Puffs. Being puffed up with pride is one thing—being trapped in Cocoa Puffs is quite another—a horror story in itself. Once Swami lured someone into the box and literally thumped him until his contents settled and he fell asleep. But that's another story.

Halloween

You may find it hard to believe, but Swami Z likes to go trick-or-treating on Halloween. He has many bed sheets from which to choose, thanks to me. Yesterday I came in from the grocery to find him sitting in the rocking chair wearing a sheet over his head. I said the only thing that I could, "Well, that's an improvement." Swami would have looked at me sadly, except that he hadn't cut any eyeholes in the sheet as yet. As it was, he just said, "So you wanth be mmmpth out of my pmnukk."

"What?" I said. "Take that stupid sheet off!" He dragged the sheet from his head, causing the few hairs on his head to stand upright.

"So you won't be eating out of my pumpkin," he repeated. He knew that I had a fondness for any kind of candy—so he could afford to say this. I had every intention of picking through his pumpkin immediately after he got it filled and brought it home. You may not think that this is a guru-disciple issue, but indeed it is. I have plenty of uncooked karmic seeds and most of them are dipped in chocolate. He had me by the short hairs of my neck and he knew it.

Swami and I were in a spiritual standoff regarding eyeholes in my bed sheets. As clumsy as he was, he would not get far without them. I would not get far without some Snickers, M&M's and Almond Joys. There must be a way to compromise on this issue, but there is no such thing as compromising with the guru.

The rest of the day went on without a reference to this thorny issue, but the following morning brought an unexpected resolution. I walked into the kitchen where Swami was eating a bowl of Cocoa Puffs and said, quite generously, "Here is a sheet that you may indeed cut eyeholes in—and you don't have to let me eat out of your pumpkin."

17

He didn't speak for a moment, due to a mouthful of Cocoa Puffs, but when he did, it was music to my ears. "I have decided not to go as a ghost, but as one of my disciples, you! I will be wearing one of your skirts and a blouse." I would like to say that I decked him, but I fought the impulse to be quite that aggressive. When I went to the closet to get the skirt and blouse for him, I felt quite satisfied. Swami has never looked good in pink and my skirt—well, it will make him look hippy.

The Teacher is Always with You

Swami Z has been hard for me to shake lately. It started with the Halloween sheet business and continues to escalate. Between you and me, I think that he is eating too much sugar. He is making Snickerdoodles for next week. My kitchen smells like cinnamon and has the "stickies." He has spilled dough in different places and never cleans it up. Some gurus tie cats to trees when they meditate. Swami sprinkles sugar 24/7. It's a wonder that we don't have more bugs in the house.

My cookie sheets are never around when I want them and Swami Z—well, what can I say? The guru is not only within, he is without. I am writing a song called, "I Can't Miss You 'Til You're Gone." Don't get me wrong—when he is *in absentia*, I am miserable. And when he is always here, I am also miserable. The student is in overload at all times. He reads my mind like it was *The New York Times*; most of it he isn't interested in. If I had coupons, he would clip them because he is very pragmatic, believe it or not.

"Vicki," he will say, causing me to startle, "did you remember to put my sheets on tumble dry, low?" I normally put everything on medium and since he is a medium, he knows that. (A little guru word play.)

"No, Swami, I put everything on medium," I remind him, beginning to gather a head of irritated steam.

"Okay, okay," says Swami cheerfully, "I will just sprinkle a little water and put them back in the dryer."

"Christened sheets," I said sarcastically. "Holy smoke."

He grabbed me and swung me around in an impromptu dance of

joy. I surrendered to the charm of this old coot, I mean *cook*. We ran out of breath and sat collapsed at the kitchen table. He took prasad from the cookie jar (pumpkin spice cookies) and fed it to me with a cup of steamed milk. I will regret this when I step on the scales, but come to think of it, with Swami, most things stay in balance.

War

Testily, I told Swami that he was my creation and I would get him a T-shirt that said, "Intellectual Property of Vicki Woodyard."

"I will get my own," he said, "One that says, 'I'm with Stupid.'"

"You can't teach!" I said.

"You can't learn," he shot back.

There is an eternal war between guru and disciple. We have put our war paint on and we are camera-ready. We can appear anywhere at any time doing anything because we don't exist. We are mere fabrications of fun and futility. We can arm-wrestle, mud-wrestle, make mud pies and sling mud at each other. I actually think that he is gearing up for a publicity tour. Advertising himself like some Streisand about to warble wisdom—for a price. I hope that never happens. He is actually too innocent for this world. Much like the Little Prince, I am his sheep and he is caring for me. Underneath my bravado I am beginning to fear that he will disappear.

Right now my true feelings for the guru are showing and I must quickly cover them up. Uh-oh, here he comes again. I put on my best "just don't get it" face and accuse him of being a charlatan. "You," I said, "are trying to pull the wool over my eyes. You're no guru. You're just playing to the crowd and they don't care about you. They would just as soon listen to somebody who makes sense—somebody who can really enlighten them, not just tease them about it."

He crossed his eyes at me and I chased him out of the room with my broom. He would vote me off of the island in a minute, and I know he wouldn't think twice.

Just a Device

I tried to tell Swami that he is just a device—a way for me to do my thing. He looked at me pathetically. I looked back at him defiantly. "Do you know this to be true?" he said, challenging my underlying assumptions as easily as a Gangaji or a Byron Katie.

"Of course," I said. "I am in total control of my thoughts. I created you out of my thoughts and I can delete you in an instant. I try to give you all the best lines," I offered. I bowed to him, ad libbing humility.

"Ah, you're just phoning me in," he said. "You are writing my character with one hand tied behind your back."

"What did you say?" I entered into the computer.

"Toss me a koan—what is the sound of one hand typing behind your back?" he said.

"I made you and I can break you," I typed.

I had him reply caustically, "You are so powerful."

I turned off the computer and stomped out of the room. While I had been yelling at him, he had stuck a "Kick Me" sign on my back. What's a mother to do! I tried to explain to Swami that he is a piece of fiction—a figment of my fevered imagination. He would have none of it.

"See," I said, pointing to the computer screen. "There's just a blank screen with a blinking cursor until I put the words down. Don't you know how actors always refer to the writers when they are accepting rewards? 'If it's not on the page,' they say with humility, feigned or otherwise."

"If you're not on the page, you don't get face time," I said threateningly. Swami is being typed quickly into a snit.

"You stupid disciples just don't get it. The guru and the disciple rise and fall together. They're like ham and eggs, peanut butter and jelly!" said Swami. We looked at each other, salivating from similes. I made us a peanut butter sandwich and backed us out of the computer and out of a potentially dangerous situation. I see a food fight in our future.

Naptime

Swami and I nap between one and two every day; that is how we stay young. The world may be going to hell in a handbasket during that time, but we are blissfully unaware. Save your hell for after a nap and you will be able to handle it better.

Swami is, after all, The Sleeping Teacher. I called him that in the beginning to let you know that he was a funny character that I had dreamed up. Was I ever wrong. When I conjured up Swami, I was summoning the Inner Teacher and he arrived wearing a bed sheet and looking ridiculous. That is how love is disguised. But back to naptime.

The ZZZs are heard as Swami quickly drops off to sleep. In the other room I am thinking of what to have for dinner and what day I should go to the grocery. My mind takes its usual route to sleep and I tag along until it finally gives up and gives me an hour's peace. When we meet in the kitchen for tea, we are ready to face the remainder of the day—with cookies washed down with tea. Enlightenment is a by-product.

More Than Anything

More than anything, Swami Z is a scent. Smelling like vanilla must be a sure sign of gurudom because Swami attracted me by his scent. Often I experience the guru's oneness as an aroma, nothing more. When I try to pin the scent down, it floats away. Yet when I seek nothing for myself, the scent comes to me unbidden and lingers in my hair. His teachings are like that, too.

He is obsessed with home to the point of idiocy. He says that he moved in with me because my little house attracted him and my suffering opened the door. He sits in the kitchen most of the time, blending wisdom with whatever he happens to be doing in there. He also likes to sit by the fire in the fall and winter, occasionally sharing an insight that he knows I am unready to hear. Then he sits back and enjoys my consternation.

"You know, don't you, that I came to live with you because I needed a roof over my head," he reminded me one late fall afternoon. "I had run out of places to stay. Everyone had kicked me out. No one is as gracious as you." He was clearly playing me for a fool.

"Now, Swami, that is just so not the truth," I hmmphed. "You told me that you moved in with me because you liked that my sheets were of such high quality—that they made wonderful outfits for you." The little man with the dough just sat there, giving me plenty of rope with which to hang myself. It is said that when the pupil is ready, the master appears. That is definitely true. And mine appears to be crazy. But no mind, I belong to him now and he belongs to me. I guess that makes us two of a kind, but what kind I don't know. Swami Z looked at me and suggested a game of poker.

"I think your content has settled," I remarked.

"Not to worry, every ounce is still there," he shot back, offering me a handful of Cocoa Puffs. We often ate them on the side. For example, for dinner we might have pasta with Puffs, or pepperoni pizza with a side of cereal. My teeth were being cut on the daily dharma that went crunch, which reminded me, I had a dental appointment. When Swami first told me that dental karma was the worst, I bit.

"Why is that, Swami?" I said, running my tongue over my lower teeth.

"Because your teeth are hard on the outside and soft on the inside, just like you. You don't know how bad the pain is until something goes wrong. Then you drill and drill until—voilà—rot." I hate to tell you that he enjoyed telling me this, but he did. I can't figure out if his teeth are false or real. He never lets me get that close to him. He is like vanilla in that if you get an actual taste of him, pure and undiluted, you will find him unsavory. He must be mixed throughout before he becomes the most useful. I bow to him and his scintilla of truth—maybe he doesn't even have that. I am the most deluded disciple that he has. Just ask him.

Attracted to Shiny Objects

"If I'm a device, then you're a—gizmo!"

Swami Z

Swami and I sat at the kitchen table. He was drinking tea and I was cleaning out the junk drawer. There were rubber bands, threadbare pot holders, matchbooks, a little steel ruler, twine, etc. We regarded the mess stoically. I picked out an ancient red jelly bean and popped it into my mouth.

Thinking that he hadn't seen me, I realized that Swami had found the perfect way to rag on me. "Got the red one at last, huh?" he said. "That jelly bean has been ruler of the junk drawer for years now and you have eaten it. Who will lead the other junk? Who will be in charge?"

"I have assimilated it," I said stiffly. "It has become a part of me. My inner junk is jumping for joy. At last, the red bean has landed."

Swami said, "Not so fast." He stood up and brought the drawer beside the one I had just cleaned out. He dumped it out on the table. There were more matchbooks, rolls of tape, instruction booklets for household appliances, and a black jelly bean. Swami popped it into his mouth triumphantly. "Checkmate," he said.

There's just no winning with Swami Z. He will go down in history as the guru who will stop at nothing to stay one up on a disciple. I couldn't wait to bring the third drawer over to the table. I knew something that he didn't—there was Ex-Lax in there.

At Swami's Table

I sat slumped over the table altogether disheartened. The holidays are bearing down and, as usual, I never seem to jump into the flow and enjoy them as they were meant to be enjoyed. I always blame commercialism, but that is just a concept, after all. Who knows, perhaps I would just skip the holidays this year—no tree or turkey or gifts—just raw honesty. I dropped my head onto the table and fell asleep.

I awoke to the smell of vanilla and saw Swami standing over me, naked little ankles and all. He wore house slippers and a warm plaid robe that I had given him last year. He had a potholder in one hand and with the other he held a box of light brown sugar. "This sugar is hard," he said, accusingly. "All lumps and hard edges—how can I bake cookies?"

I spoke before engaging my brain. "I can't do everything," I said, with about two tablespoons of self-pity.

"You got that right," said Swami. "In fact, you can't do anything!"

I looked at him with a jaundiced eye. "Looka here, Swami-doodle," I said condescendingly. "Who do you think pays the bills around here?" He eyed me silently. I eyed him back. His silence was a teaching that I will not soon forget. In silence I got up from my chair and found a piece of bread. "Here," I said, "put this in the box of brown sugar and it will soften up before you know it." Those were some of the softest cookies that Swami ever baked. And my heart—well, of course it had been softening all along. I just had a bit of a setback that afternoon.

Making Sense of Christmas

I am having trouble making sense of Christmas. Swami Z is whizzing around the kitchen baking cookies from early morning until late at night. He has cinnamon sugar on his nose and flour on his chin. Me, I'm getting grumpier by the hour. "Swami," I said, "do you not intend to wash a single dish today?" I looked at all of the cookie sheets, mixing bowls, and measuring spoons heaped high in the sink.

"Probably not," he said, biting into a warm cookie; "that's what I have you for." I must confess that having a little Swami live in your house is a bit confusing. He throws confetti on the bathroom rug and writes "I love myself" in shaving cream. He stands in front of the mirror bowing and smiling. Sometimes late at night I hear him laughing in the kitchen quite alone. At other times, he is secretive and subversive. I don't intend to let him get away with things, but that is the way it is. Occasionally he takes the bus and disappears for the day, coming home at night looking powerful and sad. I think he visits people that I will never know, taking them sweets and giving darshan to old trees.

As aggravating as he can be at times, I cannot imagine my life now without the diminutive little cookie freak. The hollow places in me are often filled with light and levity and I find myself giggling unexpectedly or crying healing tears. "I love you, Swami," I said sincerely, rising to put my arms around him before going to get dressed. He turned as red as a cherry on one of his cookies and vanished into thin air. I knew that he would reappear again when the oven timer went off. Some things you just know.

The Journey Without Distance

Swami and I sat in silence this morning for a long time. Today's silence was different. It was as if we joined ourselves in such depths that the heights were found in them. "Going down into your consciousness is the same as going up," said Swami when we had at last resumed our everyday minds. He took off his cardigan and hung it on the back of his chair. I poured hot tea for the two of us.

Lately he looks like a skinny old cherub *sans* halo. His cookies, in fact, were angel-shaped for the holidays and were piling up in my old tins. They wouldn't last long because people were beginning to seek Swami out and they never left without cookies. Rarely did people want the recipe; they wanted Swami's presence along with them. So I toted in large bags of flour and bottles of vanilla. My old swami smelled heavenly. "Today I have invited someone I met to come over," said Swami, rising from his chair. To tell the truth, I preferred keeping him to myself. Once word got out that he was so dear, there would be increasing numbers of people showing up for darshan.

I felt some trepidation as I saw an old blue Ford pulled up at the curb and in the house sat a woman deep into Swami chat. He looked up when I came in, but said nothing. He was a good listener. I don't know what they talked about, but she left with a baggie full of cookies. "She was here because her mind was giving her much trouble," said Swami, as if to ward off my jealousy. "Her mind is like yours—prone to jealousy and wild imaginings."

"So what did you tell her?" I said as I put away a few groceries and sat down to face him across the table.

"Just that the mind would not cease to give her troubles, but

since she was not the mind, she should never be afraid of it, or to call it names. I encouraged her to call it duplicitous and self-doubting."

"Well, Swami," I said, "name-calling is not such a nice thing to do, is it?"

"Never you mind," said Swami with a soft smile. "The mind is not so nice itself. It will rise up and talk back to her and then she will come to me for further advice. This time I will agree with her—and you—that the mind is not so nice. And then we sit in silence and all will be well."

Swami and I disappeared for a few moments and yet we went nowhere. When we got back, we were still absent. I knew that the journey without distance was possible and required no guidebook or map.

Christmas Eve with Swami

It is Christmas Eve and Swami and I are sitting down to a pre-bedtime supper. The old wooden table is greasy with oils and butter. Christmas placemats cover some of the spots and we are using paper cups to hold our egg nog. Swami is looking resplendent tonight in his plaid bathrobe and fur slippers. He has been up since sunrise baking the most beautiful cookies. They are arranged on an old glass plate that my grandmother gave me. There are stars and gingerbread men, green trees and red Santas wondrous to behold.

I loved Swami down to his socks. I loved him as he ate his franks and beans. I raised my paper cup to him and stood to bow and say "Namaste." Before you could say "Rudolph," he had raised my kundalini and lowered my expectations of having another question answered. I knew when to hold 'em and when to fold 'em. But I was a sheep of his fold and that is, after all, the most important thing.

We turned in early on Christmas Eve. He is clearly tired from weeks and weeks of making his beautiful cookies and hand-delivering them all over town. We had not had much time to talk about anything meaningful. Our conversation had been limited to, "Where's the flour scoop and the extra butter?" I had kept busy sweeping up his messes and going to the store for raisins, dried fruits, and chocolate chips. Now we were as whipped as the cream on his pumpkin tarts.

I turned out the lights and fell into bed exhausted. It was cold so I got up to get an extra blanket from the hall closet. If I had not seen it, I would not have believed it. Golden light was coming out from under Swami's closed bedroom door. I stepped a little closer to it and it didn't go away. Summoning my courage, I put my hand on the doorknob and opened it a crack. Swami lay on

his back, gently snoring under an old faded quilt. He was bathed in this wonderful light that now filled the room and filled my heart as well. A tear slipped down my cheek and I silently closed the door. Who's to say whose little Swami he is. Does it really matter?

The Flimsiest Day of the Year

Swami was late getting up this morning, but then so was I. December 26 is the flimsiest day of the year, strength-wise. The sun was watery and pale and I felt that way myself. Last night when I saw the light coming from under Swami's door, I had been changed against my own will. I had quickly put on my nightgown and tucked myself into bed. Shivering from the light, I had prayed for understanding and received none. How could such a scrawny little man be possessed of such power? And why had he kept it hidden from me? Didn't he know that I was avid for enlightenment? Of course he did.

I put the kettle on and buttered some toast. Spreading orange marmalade, I mused about what would happen when Swami swept into the kitchen. So far I had heard nary a peep from him. I ate my toast and washed up a few dishes. "Vicki!" said Swami suddenly. I looked up and saw nothing but my usual little comrade in cookie-baking. "Have you seen my slippers?" he asked.

"No, Swami," I said. "Aren't they beside your bed?"

"No, they're nowhere to be seen."

It was then I noticed that he was wearing an odd little pair of bed socks with a pom pom at the heel. "No matter," he said. "They'll turn up sooner or later."

Several times I almost got up the courage to ask him about the light, but the light itself seemed to stop me. As if it knew that once I asked, I would be cheating myself out of something vital. I had been doing that all of my life. Well, actually, it is beginning to feel like it is not quite my life anymore. Not since Swami moved in.

What Do You Want Me To Do?

Swami Z and I were seated at the kitchen table, elbows propped. The New Year was at our doorstep and now I asked him this question, "What do you want me to do?"

Swami Z peered into his mostly-empty teacup and said wryly, "It is best that I not tell you tonight." I was not surprised at this lack of a specific answer. Vagueness was his stock-in-trade. In the morning I got up early and put the kettle on. I tied an apron around my waist and pushed the curtains back. The day was glittering and I was quickly lost in wonder. A squirrel dashed across the lawn, as if on his way to a cache of acorns he just remembered. Swami swept into the room suddenly. He was dressed to go out, even though it was barely 9:00 a.m.

"Where are you going so early?" was my obvious question. He smiled at me and then unexpectedly came over and gave me a gentle hug. "I'm going to Macy's." I waved a plate of donuts at him and he grabbed one and sat down. I reached for his blue cup and poured hot water over a tea bag.

"I have some devotees that are expecting to see me. Before Christmas they asked me the same question that you did last night."

"Oh," I said. "What do you want me to do—that one?"

"That very one," he said, biting into the tasty circle. "I am going to tell them the same thing I tell you. You are asking the wrong question. You should be asking how you can quit asking that question. It's mental." He went on, wiping crumbs from his mouth. "Surrender never asks. It waits and then does the will of the moment. That's all."

Of course I was totally deceived by the simplicity of his answer and the test arose with my next breath. It WAS my next breath. But was it really mine?

Smelling Like Vanilla

This morning I found Swami sitting in the old rocker reading the after-Christmas sales and clearance ads. He pointed to a pair of long johns and frowned. "Itchy, scratchy," was his comment. I looked at this old man with the exceedingly skinny legs and giggled from picturing him in such a getup. "I know what you need, Swami," I said. "You need a soft flannel shirt from L.L.Bean, maybe something in a red plaid."

"L.L.Bean," he said. "Yes, that's the ticket. Get me a red plaid flannel shirt. It'll look good with my jeans and mala. I'll go to Macy's Sleep Department and sign bed sheets and look with-it, look hip."

"Okay, now you're making fun of me," I said. "Go ahead, wear your ratty old bed sheet and play Swami to the hilt. You do it very well." I could feel my blood pressure rising. Didn't the old man know what was good for him? The last time I saw him he was going out the door on the way to Macy's. He was wearing one of my 350-count cotton sheets and smelling like vanilla. Sheesh!

A New Year

Swami Z has been gone all afternoon. I have taken a nap and taken down the Christmas tree. Boxing up the old ornaments, I smiled at how happy Swami had made me this past year. He moved in about a year ago and most of my projects have fallen by the wayside. That is as you would suspect; for no one can accommodate a Swami readily. Swami Z has required me to take a new look at how I live my life. Making room for his baking projects has taken up a lot of time. Grumbling at how messy he was, at first I resisted cookie-baking with all of my might. But soon the aroma of vanilla had me hooked. I have been looking forward to a fresh January batch.

My waistband has gotten a little tighter; yet Swami remains as slender as ever. He is looking healthy these days. Maybe it is because he walks most everywhere he goes. Sometimes he takes the bus, but the stop is only a few blocks from our house. The lines between truth and fiction have definitely faded since Swami moved in. I used to think that my thoughts were real and that I had made Swami up. Now I know that my thoughts are unreal and only He is. Paradox comes in many different packages. Speaking of which, I hear the front door opening. "Swami, is that you?"

"No," he called out, "it's the Big Bad Wolf." I better go and let him in before he blows the house down.

Be What You Are

Swami Z waltzed around the kitchen with the broom. I eyed him wearily, finally saying, "Ah, knock it off." My guru looked askance at me. I mean, what has the world come to when one is smart-alecky with the very fount of wisdom? I didn't care. January had kicked me in the seat of the pants and they were already two sizes too small. Not to mention my heart. I felt as Grinchy as I looked. My mirror had been telling me that I was fat and now Swami was throwing good cheer in my face. How much worse could it get? Life hates a smart aleck and finds ways of teaching it humility. Swami Z was the present agent doling it out to me.

"Vicki," he said, "what's eating you? Or should I say, what have you been eating?"

"Junk," I said. "I've been eating junk—that you fix. Cookies, cookies, cookies."

"That's not fair," said Swami. "You know good and well we only eat cookies when we have cleaned our plates—eaten our vegetables and drunk our milk." He was right, the little doofus!

"I'm depressed," I spat the words out like watermelon seeds.

"You coulda fooled me," said Swami. "I thought you were high on life." Sarcasm is Swami's middle name. He was not going to let me get away with anything, but continued. "Why do you think I came here to live with you? To support you in your old ways, to let you compromise your integrity, to get you off the hook? No, indeed. I am here to goad you into being what you already are."

"And what's that?" I said, weary with winter and all of its lack of light.

"I am here to pull the rug out from under you and believe me, that is no easy job."

I stood up so I could look him right in the eye. "Okay, go ahead," I said, throwing down the gauntlet.

"You are no good to yourself or anyone else the way you are. You march right back to the path and get going," was his reply.

"It's disappeared," I wailed.

"No, it's right where you left it," snapped Swami. "Now get going." I disappeared into my depression like a snowflake on a hot stove. Swami would know the next step to take.

The Ankles of a Swami

There is something about Swami's ankles that are the dearest thing about him. I suppose it's the way they poke out of his fuzzy slippers when he scurries about the kitchen late at night. They are scrawny, pale and downright silly.

I always fear that Swami will withdraw his love, leaving me in the lurch. Is that the root of my human fears and emotions toward this apparition of a guru—and does he know me better than I know myself?

I see him as a quasi-Swami, quicksilver and mysteriously mine. Yet his love is obviously a shoreless ocean, as someone once described another saint. Oh, yes, I do believe that he is a saint, albeit a little overdone around the edges. His barks and squeaks and hollers are nothing but subterfuge to keep me thinking that he is the same as me. Lord, I hope not.

Just as I begin to re-emerge from my musings, the little guy sails past. "On my way to the Dollar Store," he hollers at me as the door bangs behind him. "Got to get some cookie cutters and they should be on sale."

He never asks if I need anything, the inconsiderate old—never mind. I was trying to see if you were paying attention. You know I love him, don't you?

Soliloquy

*"Have confidence; obey without asking questions.
In this way the being will come to have priority over the ego."*

Lizelle Reymond

"Swami," I said, as we sat in front of the fire in the living room, "I don't understand anything about you." He cracked a crooked smile and opened his crinkly old eyelids, saying nothing. He pulled a blue afghan over his feet that were propped up on the footstool.

"When you first came here to live, I thought you were a *bona fide* nutcase, but a funny one. Remember how you stood over me at the computer and interrupted my train of thought? Here, have some popcorn."

I passed him the bowl and went on talking. He put it down, obviously no more hungry than I was. "All things considered, I think I owe you an apology," I said. "I mean, you are one of the sanest people that I know—not that that's saying a lot." I thought about my family and how conflicted we all were. Swami's conflicts always had a purpose to them. If he drove me crazy, it was to make me acknowledge how mixed up I was and how much I suffered.

"And when you left for a while, I grieved as if you had died. What was that all about?" I queried. "Didn't you know how much I had come to rely on you?" The fire crackled and spit and I heard the clock strike ten. "I know that once I welcomed you back, things seemed to have undergone an alchemical change. I stopped resisting your odd schedule and began to look forward to your bursting through the kitchen door. My loneliness, thanks to you, is becoming more alone and—spiritual. Maybe it's aloneness. I know that everyone suffers and wants to have love in a demonstrable form."

42

"Swami," I said impetuously. "Please don't leave me—not now. Just when I am beginning to know you." The old guy had fallen asleep. I pulled the afghan up under his chin and kissed the top of his head—and went to get my camera.

Yoga with Swami Z

Just before his death Shakyamuni said,
"I have taught nothing at all!"

Swami Z is vacuuming right now and it is so noisy that it is hard for me to think. Last night I was trying to think of a way to go about asking him to teach me yoga, but he talked me into popcorn instead. He is quite limber, doing the cobra just as it should be done. My body could use some tuning up. Everyone is overloading the gyms this month, so I don't want to go that route.

"Vicki," said Swami, dragging the vacuum and storing it in the hall closet, "get your yoga mat and we'll begin." I was all excited until I realized that he was going to pop a yoga DVD in and leave me alone! The little guy was gonna put me in someone else's virtual hands. Sheesh. As the video began to play, I watched intently but my attention was partly focused on Swami. He had lain down on the couch and was snoring away. ZZZZZZ does not half describe it. It was more like a ZZZZZZ to the nth power. The glass on the end table was quivering. He was not much of an example right this minute.

See, that's the problem with having a live-in guru. The shoemaker's children's feet go bare. You get the picture. When Swami is at Macy's, he spouts his best lines. At home, I have no such luck. He is more likely to discuss Snickerdoodles and Ding Dongs. Right now the freezer is crammed with peanut butter cookies and gingerbread. I made it through all 45 minutes of the yoga tape before deliberately drawing a face on his little bald head as he slept. It was pretty good if I do say so myself. The art of living with a little Swami turns up in the oddest places!

Karmic Seeds

Swami and I are eating karmic seeds for dinner. They don't taste very good, especially if you have to keep eating leftovers. For instance, on Monday night we had Family Fights and then again on Thursday and Saturday. You can't get these meals in a red box at the supermarket. They just show up unexpected and unannounced. They seem to multiply in your mouth and leave lots of leftovers for successive nights.

What do Swami and I fight about? Before I tell you that, let me hasten to explain that Swami is the one who decides which seeds we will be heating up; all I can do is eat them. He likes to serve me ignorance over and over again. That is because I am an intellectual and use words to defend myself.

He is constantly leaving crumb trails throughout the house and sometimes he mixes anger seeds in with them. I blow up and bang! We are off to the family fight. When I accuse him of being messy, he counterattacks with the fact that I am a perfectionist. I launch into a verbal attack on his purpose in making me angry. "Vicki, Vicki, Vicki," he said, brushing crumbs from his flannel shirt, "don't you know that you can't change anyone but yourself?"

"Of course I do," I snorted, "but if you're so enlightened, why are you such a slob?" I stopped and looked at him; at his diminutive figure and almost helpless demeanor. I wanted to hug him and hit him at the same time. He is paradox perfected. I didn't wait for him to answer. I turned on my heel and left the room, which guaranteed that we would be eating leftovers tomorrow night. Swami will not rest until all of my seeds are cooked.

Valentine's with Swami

Swami Z had just pulled a sheetful of cookies from the oven. I couldn't wait to eat my share. I had learned, however, that Swami did not take kindly to people eating the cookies right off the sheet. He liked to present them on a milk glass plate that had belonged to my mother. He discovered it shortly after he moved in and promptly appropriated it. Memories now mingled with the smells of cinnamon and vanilla. We sat across from each other at the bare table—salt and pepper shakers pushed out of the way. I thought this boded well for what I had to ask Swami once I ate a warm cookie or two.

"Swami," I said, swallowing the last melt-in-your-mouth morsel, "could you please tell me how I can become more loving?" He looked up at the ceiling. The silence began and continued until I was about ready to leave. When he spoke, his words were unusually slow.

"Do you love me?" he asked. "Or do you love yourself loving me?" Of course, such a question could never have a logical answer. He knew that—the old poop. "And do I have to earn your love—or does it come free with no strings attached?" I looked up at the ceiling myself.

"No, Swami, you don't have to earn my love. How could you? It just arises, sort of like your cookies as they bake." I got up my courage to go on. "And the part about loving myself loving you—that's just a conundrum."

"A whatzit?" he snapped, doing his testy old man bit. "Is that anything like a poser?"

"Sort of. If I loved myself loving you, would that be such a bad thing?"

"It wouldn't be the real deal," he sighed. "You know I never use imitation vanilla. And if I did, I would only do it in an emergency. In fact, I would use lemon extract first."

"What does that have to do with how I can become more loving?"

He didn't hesitate a New York minute before saying nothing. The conversation was coming from the wrong place and he was putting me in mine. Love was just going to have to take a backseat to more important things like flavorings. I rolled my eyes, knowing that this was turning from love to cookies. It didn't really matter. I had been given Valentine's prasad by the master chef. The next thing I knew, Swami was talking about using almond flavoring if he had run out of lemon extract. What exactly is a devotee to do?

Are You Having a Fresh Experience?

"Swami," I said with a heavy sigh, "I feel so guilty for all of the things I've done—and haven't done." He looked at me with great energy in his eyes—as if he had just been given an unexpected gift. What was that about? He said nothing but went to the spice rack and with a grand gesture, waved his arm, causing them to fall wildly onto the floor.

"Such a noise," he said. "Almost unendurable." He took an apple from the wooden bowl and examined it closely. Having satisfied himself that it was fresh, he took it to the sink, washed it and sat down. He took a large bite, smiling with satisfaction. "Now that's an experience," he said smugly. I wanted to hit him.

Then Comes the Silence

Swami is a relentless cookie-baker. He is busy from morning until night, pursuing his passion for freshness. He gives these cookies away to one and all. I have seen him invent a new recipe and give it away before the cookies had cooled off. He has total faith in his ability to please the senses. Now why would that matter? I have often wondered. To be the recipient of a batch of his cookies is to understand the power of unconditional love. Forget the Pillsbury Dough Boy—I have the Swami of the Sugar Cookie living at my house. His spatula should be bronzed and hung in The Cookie Hall of Fame.

If you are a milk-drinker, they are wonderful washed down with a tall, cold glass. They also go well with hot chocolate or ginger tea. Should you ever be lucky enough to sit at Swami's table, don't discount something known as the Mystery. It is baked into every bite and hits you like a ton of bricks. The first time that Swami fed me a cookie, I knew that he was more than he appeared to be. He was giving me prasad straight from the Master Chef. All I could do was bow and lick my lips. Had I known what was to come, I would have packed up and left. For with each bite of cookie, I have found myself steadily disappearing. And it's not easy.

I have cried over what Swami has asked me to do. And what is that, you are wondering? It has something to do with loving someone beyond yesterday and tomorrow. It involves moving into empty space and being unable to decorate it with anything familiar. Then comes the silence.

The Wings of a Swami

I have been chasing Swami around with my mental butterfly net for far too long. He is achingly beautiful and I do what I can to capture him so that I can get a closer look. You are saying, "What do you mean, achingly beautiful? Are you referring to his skinny ankles or one of his sparse hairs?" Of course not. Swami's beauty arises from somewhere that I have never been. It is as much a scent as anything. It causes me to stop and look at him from the corner of my heart. He may be standing at the kitchen counter mixing dough or just sitting quietly in front of the fire. He knows that he does this to me and he laughs. "Swami," I said, "why is it that you aggravate me and activate my heart chakra at the same time?"

"Never question love," he shot back, almost angrily. As if to stress his meaning, he spun around and looked at me full in the face. I looked back and the spell was broken. Now I saw what he meant. Something had evaporated and it wasn't vanilla. It was an imperceptible movement between us. I had done this—had broken a delicate cobweb spun of faith. Dagnabbit!

I put the kettle on and sat waiting for it to whistle. Swami took off his apron and washed his hands. He came over to me and took both of my hands in his. He turned them palms up and kissed each one. I wondered. This was not in Swami's usual repertoire. I said nothing. The moment remained.

All I Saw Was Everything

I had a question for Swami and sat waiting for him to reappear for dinner. I had fixed franks and beans and biscuits from the can. Believe it or not, Swami didn't object to fast food, whether cooked at home or brought in. Perhaps it is his antidote to stress, I don't know. He breezed in around 6:00 and we ate, as usual, without saying too much. After cleaning up the kitchen, I asked Swami my question. "Swami, what do you think about me doing what you do—you know, speaking to people about the truth?"

He rolled his eyes before letting a weary sigh escape from his lips. "About the truth—about the truth? That's like being a little pregnant—just isn't possible." He rubbed his belly and stretched his legs before the fire. "Is you is or is you ain't my baby?" he sang—as if to emphasize the ambiguity of such a subject. I said nothing. He said nothing. The clock ticked and the DVR came on. I looked at its automatic recording of a program and Swami smiled. "You want to do a recording, huh?"

"Not exactly," I said. "I want to help people."

"No one there to help," said Swami. "Help yourself, though. That's always a good thing to do. Can't do too much of that." He got up from his chair and walked over to mine. Leaning down, he patted the top of my head and said, "See you in the morning. Sweet dreams."

That night I dreamt of Swami and me dancing under a full moon. He was young and I was old—just the reverse of our real life. It made me wonder. Suddenly it didn't seem to matter if my worth depended on helping other people. Who were they, anyway? When I looked outside my window, all I saw was everything.

51

Unreal

Today was a disturbing one for me and that's as it should be. The status quo is never a good thing. That's why knowing Swami is like knowing a river personally—just can't be done. You can admire its beauty or its power; that is something else altogether. I think that people are ultimately the same way. We must let them flow.

But back to what happened. Swami came into the kitchen early and turned the stove on. Setting the kettle on, he returned to his chair and sat in silence. I looked at him closely. He looked the same as always; his plaid bathrobe was neatly knotted and his little head was pink in the kitchen's light. "So, Vicki," he said. "I don't quite know how to say this, but I'll try." He cleared his throat in a tentative way. I regarded him as I would a statue that has come to life, which is pretty much how he happened, come to think of it.

"I know that I am not real."

I didn't know how to reply so I just sat there clumsily, almost falling out of the chair from embarrassment. I tried to make light of what he just said.

"Yeah," I said, "I guess the jig is up. I created you just to have some interesting copy on my website."

"Not only am I not real," he continued, "but it doesn't seem to matter." Tears were forming in my eyes as I reached over and patted him on his arm. I could feel the texture of his soul.

"It matters to me," I said, beginning to weep. "Look at what I've gone and done. Created a character that I have come to love and now I find out that he knows he is only a character. But there's

something even wronger than that—I want you to be real. I want it so bad I can taste it."

Swami and I are having a hard time with this one. He would like to comfort me, but how can unreality give comfort? He got up and poured hot water into his mug and returned to the table.

"Vicki," he said, reaching across and patting my hand. "Not to worry. I don't exist, but you don't either!" He had triumphed over me once again. Perhaps the game was still on.

Orphan

Swami has decided that he is an orphan and wants all of the sympathy contained therein. He is also determined that I, too, see myself in the same way. He is staging dramatic scenes revolving around our pitiful, lonely life. All that because he isn't real and neither am I. How can the unreal have parents or relatives? He continues to bake cookies and has come up with a new version of a chocolate chip. He calls them 'onlies'.

"Onlies?" I said. "What the heck kind of name is that for a cookie?"

"Better than 'lonelies,'" he shot back. He is trying (I think) to make the best of his unreality. To that end, he is rocketing around the house baking nonstop. Already he has been to the market to buy chocolate chips and butter. I enjoy this part of his hyperactivity.

"This is gonna be a good batch," he says, licking his lips. "Of course, they are only as good as you think they are. Have one." I took the warm cookie with its melted chocolate chips and said the only thing possible: "This is gooood." The word "good" looked like a stretch limo that I could ride around in. Being unreal with Swami is better than being real with the rest of the world.

Stuck

"Swami," I wailed, "I'm stuck." We were sitting in front of the fire kicking around a variety of spiritual topics. I confided that I didn't know what God wanted me to do. "I know there's some task that I've come to do—but I can't figure it out." Swami looked at his fingernails then up at the ceiling. I know him so well by now that I readied myself for a worthless answer. He was not about to give up any real info. He never had; why should he start now? Sunlight was coming in through the window—a weak, watery light that was merciful to the dust on the end tables. You could have written 'Swami' in it.

"Here it comes," he said with a certain air of feigned boredom. "I have some gift to share—some calling...."

"Yeah," I said blackly. "Is it me or is it getting sarcastic in here?" Swami stood up and stretched his back. I could hear it creaking. Then he struck his head with his hand and said, "Ah, yes, now I remember! I don't exist. You invented me and let me think that I was real. I don't have to listen to your problems."

He went on: "Let me clue you in—you don't exist either. We are awash in a sea of what some people call *samskara*. But let's get this straight. I call it egocentric thinking." He sat abruptly and tried to look irritated, but he couldn't quite pull it off. What had come over him? Yesterday he was a cuddly orphan, baking his 'onlies'.

"Snap out of it, Swami," I barked. "And get your feet off the sofa." (I always resort to being a bully when I can do nothing else.) Swami stood up, brushed off his corduroys and exited stage left. I pulled the curtains and called it a day. That night as we passed each other in the hall, it was all I could do to keep from hugging him. No matter what he did or said, I loved him

deeply. He is my bulwark in a sea of uncertainty. Let no one tell me that he does not exist. He does. I made him up. I oughta know!

PART II

"What is prayer, Swami?" Michael asked, as if he had never thought of that before.

Swami took a sip of cocoa and put his mug down precisely. "Prayer is what is left over after all the prayer words have been said," answered Swami. "You can sweep up the prayer words and leave a nice empty space for a miracle."

The Nuances of Home

"Be it ever so humble there's no place like home!"
John Howard Payne

"Swami," I said abruptly, which is never a good way to begin anything. "From now on, you and I are going to start practicing what we preach."

Swami looked up from the newspaper as if he had heard that one before. "Oh, yeah?" was his only comment. He left me no choice but to continue my soliloquy.

"There are a few people who read us just because they think we are warm and funny," I said. "And we are. It's just that, well—I can be more than that."

"Oh, I quite agree," said Swami, making it obvious that he was reading his favorite comic strip, *Mutts*. "Perhaps we can put an addition on the house and I can start giving satsang out back."

I looked at him and suddenly the lightning bolt I had waited for all of my life hit. It was like a euphoric Utopian *whee!* He had spoken and it would happen. I felt it in the tingling of my toes. My whole body felt it. The impact was immense. I had come home without ever leaving.

"Swami," I whooped. "That's it! That is exactly it! I'll call Home Depot today. I'll get somebody to draw up a plan. Ooh, this is good. This is really, really good. Just you giving everything you know to everyone who wants it."

"And what if nobody wants it?" he said dryly.

"That's easy," I shot back. "Your wisdom will be more than

58

enough for me. You'll be like loaves and fishes and I'll get the leftovers."

Swami raised a question that I didn't like the ring of, so I let the machine get it. What was the question? Stay tuned.

The Question

The question that Swami raised when I told him that I wanted him to start giving satsang to the public was this—what if they turn on you? He knew my Achilles heel—the fear of abandonment.

I did things that would provoke abandonment so I wouldn't have to be on the receiving end. I made the first obnoxious move in any situation that threatened my ego. Swami had just revealed the great flaw in my plan. I had no intention of making it work. I was priming myself for failure.

Swami's weariness with me was the real deal. He saw what was coming and didn't like what lay ahead for me. Him, he was safe. Safety doesn't worry about losing itself.

And why would I do this to an old man? He looked around the kitchen, at its warmth and coziness as if he saw the Four Horsemen about to ride through. I could have saved him from this—and I didn't.

Satsang with Swami Z

The doorbell rang before I opened both eyes. It was the Home Depot man. I let him in and we sat down at the kitchen table. "I want to build an addition on the back of the house," I said. "Big enough to have drop-in satsang." He looked at me like I had just spilled some brains out of my head and he was going to have to pick them up. "You know," I said, "drop-in satsang. Kick off your shoes and stay awhile satsang." He decided to let that comment go—to let it fly over his head.

"How big do you want it to be?" was his next question.

"Big enough for the universe and small enough so it won't be overwhelming. Swami usually manages to pull this off. Surely you can do the same."

Unfortunately Swami wandered in at that point, pulling his ratty red cardigan closed. He had a notebook in his hand. "Look what I found, Vicki," he said. "My satsang notes from the '80s."

I considered changing my mind about the whole deal. I groaned, grimaced and got the picture. Swami would be doing his thing on a regular basis. Let's listen in....

"I'm not a spiritual teacher," intoned Swami in a mock-serious way. "I'm no one in particular. I just happen—" (and here his voice grew very conspiratorial)—"to know." He assumed a mock importance and offered his hand to me as he said, "This is one of my star students."

What could I do but keep the charade going? "Yes, dear Swami, I reverence your wisdom and your ability to keep your schtick in place no matter what."

The Home Depot man couldn't have cared less. He obviously knew loonies when he saw them. "Okay, I'll draw up a plan and get back to you," he replied.

"Good, good," I said, ushering him to the door. When it closed behind him, I began to cry. "Swami, I can't do it. I've already changed my mind. I'm writing us back the way we used to be."

He looked almost real as he said softly, "Would that were possible. Would that were possible." But he didn't say that. I deleted that sentence and chose to have him say this, "Cheer up, kiddo, I'm about to make some cookies."

Surrender to the Impossible

*"I am in the universe and the universe is in me.
This is complicated."*

Swami Z

Swami and I are safe from students at the moment. The new room still smells like paint and looks like no one lives in it. But next month we are going to have satsang with Swami and have invited anybody and everybody. Swami won't tell me what he thinks will happen. He knows and is keeping me in suspense. (Translation: Vicki doesn't have a clue.)

"Let's practice," I begged Swami, hoping that something would click with me that I could write about.

"Okey dokey," said Swami at his most affable. "You pretend that you have come here to seek my guidance."

I assumed a pleading posture and sat down across from Swami at his table. "Swami, what is surrender and how can it be done?"

"You chucklehead," said Swami, in what I thought was a condescending manner. He went on, "That question is as old as the hills. I need some smart, cool, groovy questions." The way he said "groovy" reminded me of Austin Powers.

I tried again. "Swami, baby, I dig the universe, but I don't want to surrender to it. I want to keep on being me." I ran my hand over my hair in a cool manner.

Swami looked irritable and put on an inscrutable Zen master expression. He sneered and then said loudly, "Go! Next devotee. Who's next?"

I assumed the guise of Devotee Number Two. "Swami, I just want to experience your teachings and your wisdom. Let me bask in your presence."

"Don't you see the sign? No basking allowed. Well, between the hours of 8:00 and 2:00, anyway," he said a bit apologetically.

"Just give me your grace and I will leave a happy devotee," I said. Swami looked at me, momentarily forgetting that this was just a drill, and gave it to me. You should be so lucky.

The First Visitor

"This I know, that knowing nothing, unawares, the current of the cosmos's awareness flows towards you."

Rabindranath Tagore

The first visitor arrived right on schedule. I showed him into the brand spanking new satsang room and he bowed to Swami Z and handed him a flower, an artificial one. God help me. The universe sent us a ringer.

Swami was gracious, offering Fred freshly-baked cookies. (Fred is not his real name; he just uses it when he's embarrassed to be seen somewhere.)

"Fred, what can I do you for?" (I loved it when Swami used cool expressions like that.)

"Well, Swamiji, I want to know the meaning of life. Is it real?"

Swami took a cookie himself before beginning to formulate his answer. When he spoke, it looked like one of his teeth was missing. A large chocolate chip had stuck to it.

"It's like this, Fred. Life is only real when you are. Sadly, I am not real myself. Vicki just writes me and voilà—instant Swami. Gotta love it."

I was vastly and profoundly relieved. Swami had no intention of changing the way people perceived him. His public demanded stupidity and he was out to oblige. My little Swami was going to share what he didn't have with people who didn't really want it. Phew. What a relief. What a flippin' relief.

Everything Means Everything

Grace is a given when someone meets Swami. He is the very manifestation of it. Keep in mind that he is not real and you are not real and all will flow in the direction of your immense joy. Joy should be all-consuming, don't you think?

Here Swami comes now. He is entering in the style of Elvis in *Aloha from Hawaii*. The satsang crowd roars and I usher them to their seat in infinity. Swami opens with a bow and *pow!* the tiger roars. I am appalled. Three people are sitting here for the first satsang and they are all women—older women. This is gonna get ugly.

Swami, as will be his wont, asks for questions. Doris wants to know if wanting material goods is a bad thing. Poor Swami—up to his eyeballs in what he does best. This is like shooting fish in a barrel. Only in this case, Swami surprises me.

The things of the spirit have their place and you must honor that. But when the kitchen timer goes off, priorities must change. He got up to take a fresh batch of cookies from the oven. Even satsang took a backseat to cookie-baking. When you understand the rules, you can break them. The devotees sat quietly. I knew, however, that soon someone would throw a spitball. Probably at me. I hated this—I really did.

He never came back. I had to explain to Doris and the others in the room that Swami just wasn't in the mood for satsang today. I ushered them out the door and raced to the kitchen to confront Swami. He refused to discuss the matter. Does it matter?

You see, I am out of ideas for this sudden turn of events. How do you write a satsang when the one giving it leaves? I am just a typist. Frankly, I am hoping that Swami will realize how

few people really want the truth. He will let me get out of this graciously and we can return to how things used to be. Fat chance.

All or Nothing

Vicki has wandered into the satsang room where she realizes Swami has begun without her. A dozen people, many of them chubby, are listening to Swami hold forth while they are holding cookies. There are many fat grams in Swami's satsangs. "Vicki, sit down, sit down," said Swami heartily. "Someone has just asked why I picked you to live with."

I looked around at the munching devotees who were only half-listening. Kaboom! Kundalini alert. Kundalini alert! Did no one sense the power of Swami Z? If they did, they would put down those cookies and listen. "Vicki is so open that she lets just anyone come into her heart—and that is why she is so closed at the same time," Swami said. "She is a revolving door. But me, I'm a saint. I let anyone come to satsang and stay until they are full."

"Vicki and I live together and we would have started this much sooner if she had not been so filled with suffering. I had to get a dumpster to haul away a goodly portion of it. Now she knows how to work around it."

A devotee raises his hand tentatively. "Swami, I have a time-share. Would you come and stay with me for two weeks in March?"

"Absolutely not," said Swami. "It's all or nothing and Vicki knows that. She's up for the bitter and the sweet. I am changing her faster than the law allows. That is where grace comes in."

Grace was wafting through the satsang room and in and out of some listening ears. It has ever been thus.

The Curmudgeon

Swami Z is a thorough-going curmudgeon, but only when it suits him. At other times, he is a woolly little lamb. Go figure. Satsang is not the place to ask dumb questions—let me warn you in case you ever get the nerve to come. It ain't easy. Sit in the back row, keep quiet and perhaps you will experience grace. If you raise your hand and haven't formulated your questions well, God help you.

Swami has appointed me door person and I have to show people to their seats. Some days there are a dozen people stuffed in our little satsang room. They tend towards the moony-eyed star-gazing type. Looking for a guru to "luv."

"Howdy," said Swami Wayne, affecting a sudden Western drawl. What is this, *High Noon*? "Glad to see everyone," he went on. "I'll take questions if anyone has them."

There was a certain amount of shifting around of bottoms on hard metal chairs and a lot of throat clearing. Finally, someone ventured to raise a hand. Swami said, "Shoot."

The woman wanted to know if grace was possible when you don't deserve it. "That's why it's called grace," sighed Swami, showing a tinge of irritability. He must be constipated, even with the Ex-Lax.

"The only grace worth having is that of undeserved grace. Isn't that right, Vicki?" Clearly I am a perfect example. I nodded, a perfect display of hopelessness.

"Vicki didn't even know that she was using her brains to get to her heart," he giggled. "She thought I'd give her grades for getting enlightened. She wanted to do term papers and theses."

He withdrew an imaginary pistol from his imaginary holster, blew it and twirled it around. He looked at me, took aim and said softly, "Gotcha." Believe it or not, he was right. I was an insufferable fool.

Vicki's Satsang

"Vicki," said Swami, "do you think you could give satsang for me today? I've got a headache."

Well, in the first place, Swami absolutely, positively never has headaches. And in the second place, he has just stepped on my last nerve.

"Not a chance," I said, reiterating it in hopes that he would get the message. "Not a chance."

Of course the universe knows better and I found myself facing about half a dozen people in the new satsang room later that afternoon. The first question to be answered, of course, was "Where's Swami Z?" Just for meanness, I said that he was in the shower and I expected him to be out momentarily. (I knew that he was behind the door listening.) I passed around a tin of scrumptious cookies that Swami had spent all morning baking. There is nothing like a batch of warm cookies when one is facing a herd of hyenas. They were as happy as an Oprah audience that has just been given a bagful of freebies. I smiled, showing my teeth in fear. "Who has a question—just until Swami gets here," I said placatingly.

Wilma wanted to know if God was inside or outside of her. I knew that Swami Z was up on this question and that he would give her the answer in a nanosecond. Not me. I temporarily forgot who I was and God knows, that was key. Or was it? Apparently not. I glibly said that God was both inside and outside and that she was the same. Note to myself: Did we really want Wilma everywhere? Maybe she could start just being somewhere rather than everywhere. See, I am not the real deal. Only Swami is.

The flop sweat on my forehead grew. Fred, no relation to Wilma

except on God's side of the family, asked me if Swami could levitate. That was easy. "Oh, yes," I said. "I once found him stuck in the tree out in the backyard. He got just so far off the ground and then a breeze flew him into the fork of the tree." Swami, standing behind the door, winced; whether at the memory or at my answer, I do not know.

I let the rest of the satsang group grill me until I was done. Stick a fork in me—I'm enlightened. There was only one question that interested me. Where in the heck was Swami? The group of devotees was about to turn on me when Swami strolled in. He said not a word, but went straight to his work, Santa Claus guru that he is. He reached into his sack and produced a baker's dozen of his finest—chocolate chip with pecans.

Everyone in the room bonded with Swami. They quacked around the room after him like they were baby ducks being imprinted. I knew something that they didn't know. He was feeding them with the essence of himself and they would never, ever be disappointed in what he gave them. Call it enlightenment; call it unconditional love. You feel it as you read my words. That is the power of my little Swami.

Getting Down to Business

Swami and I are beginning to enjoy the satsang routine. We are getting a roomful of devotees who come to play with Swami. He always brings warm cookies and we keep the kettle on. Some days he speaks for a brief period and on others he takes questions. Here is a recent one:

"Swami, do you think that enlightenment is possible for people who really want it?" Swami heaved a sigh. This was familiar ground. He was no different than any other wise man; he lived the questions and the answers. Until you are ready to do that, nothing will change. But he met each questioner at his or her point of readiness. Today none of us was ready.

Bliss of the Self

"Satsang is nothing other than mountains meeting with mountains."

Pamela Wilson

Swami's satsangs were slowly but surely taking off. Some days we had a dozen people huddled around him in the small addition to our house. Some ladies had sewn soft cushions to put on the metal folding chairs. The men were not so creative, but were happy to do a little repair if needed. Today Swami asked for questions and it was a man who raised his hand first. "Yes, Jim," said Swami, recognizing him.

"I need to have a question answered that has been bothering me all of my life. Why aren't I happy? Spiritual teachers say that our true nature is bliss, but I don't experience that." He looked genuinely hopeful that Swami was going to give him an answer. It is ever thus. Swami is no different than any other teacher; he cannot satisfy the mind.

Swami looked softly into the devotee's eyes. Jim was a thin man dressed in polyester pants and an inoffensive shirt. He allowed himself to return the gaze. Swami sighed, encouraging Jim to sigh as well. I caught myself doing the same thing. Poor Jim.

The silence began to grow. If you were allowing yourself to receive it, you knew that it was not silence, but the bliss of the Self. Mountains meeting their mountain nature for the first time often sob softly. Jim was not about to do that, but I did it for him. I reached in my pocket for a tissue and blew my nose. Jim, however, was a different man when Swami passed out the butter cookies a little while later. I knew he was because I had changed a little more myself. Swami may be ludicrous, but he gets the job done.

Later that night I asked Swami how Jim was able to get it so quickly. He spit the answer from his mouth like watermelon seeds. "How do you know he did?"

"I could see it; I could feel it," I said. "I know that the silence brought him back to himself like words can never do."

Swami sighed. "If you could see it and feel it, why can't you live it?" I had no answer for that question.

The Bic Guru

Swami claims to have enlightened more than his share. Rose and Jim and a few others are now flicking their Bics when he says something especially overwhelming. They are pushovers for his patter. "I cannot enlighten anyone for I am no one." Yeah, right. All he has to do is brandish his spatula and disciples come running. I am feeding an army of goofy people who never wash the dishes. They can lick the bowl, but they can't load the dishwasher. I am getting fed up.

Jim has taken to quoting Swami right in the middle of the Sears appliance section, where he works. He has been heard to recommend that people buy washers and dryers and then come to satsang. I am running out of folding chairs. Swami has nothing to say to drop-ins of this ilk. So why does he invite them? Beats me.

A man who had just bought a washer-dryer combo came to satsang and raised his hand. Turns out he had a lint-trap question. And here I have been trapped in concepts for most of my life—apparently that is nothing compared to lint. Swami gave him satori, kensho and change for a dollar. The man left happy and with a baggie of cookies. I rest my case. Satsang over! Now shoo!

Breakdown

Swami and I sat in the sun waiting for the first satsang attendee to show. I cried softly. Someone that I knew was quite ill and if I didn't let the sorrow out, I wouldn't have room for healing space in my heart. Swami knew that. He started to speak to me, but then Jim and Rose wandered in together and they were clearly in a happy mood. Swami patted the top of my head, saying softly, "It's gonna be okay." Michael, Sam and Larry sat down and a few others—then Swami began to speak. It was not at all what I expected to hear.

"Listen, you people," shouted Swami at the top of his lungs. "Whoever told you that satsang is something you attend? Satsang is what you are!" With one body we all cringed. Swami thundered on. "I am sick and tired of you people coming here to receive my darshan, my cookies, my, my—" he sputtered in what appeared to be anger—"my time! All I ever wanted was to embody the truth—and I get this! This crowd of cookie-eating, self-satisfied, waiting-for-the-punch-line, spiritual wannabes!" I knew that this was the worst epithet that Swami could come up with.

He continued, "Your adoration of me will be cold comfort when your time comes—when the stuff hits the fan for you!" Jim was wincing and Rose was cowering. They missed the fact that this was not the reaction that Swami was looking for. Apparently none of us had it. That night Swami came over to where I sat huddled under an afghan on the couch and handed me a mug of tea. "Still miserable, huh?" said Swami.

"I guess you could say that," I said. "My best friend may be dying. Nothing anyone can do."

Swami looked at his hands. He looked beyond me into the night. "Why do you think I came to live with you? To help you

through the good times?" He looked old, pained, and fragile as hell. "There are some sorrows that even you cannot lift," I said, hoping that he would correct me as usual.

"Quite right," said Swami. "God is into heavy lifting, not me." He looked at me and gave me a crooked grin.

"Swami, why did you yell at everyone who came to satsang today?"

"Did I?" he asked. "I thought I was inviting them to go higher, go deeper. I forget that they prefer to see me through shallow eyes."

"It's not that," I said, in defense of those who loved Swami like I did. "It's just that you attacked them without warning."

"Just like life—I came at them just like life. Raw, hard-hitting, and true."

The next satsang went as usual. The air had been cleared. Swami was running the satsang straight down the road and all of its occupants were on board. My friend, however, was still ill. For that friend, I dedicate this satsang.

Nothing Ever Changes

Q. What makes us progress?
A. Silence is the main factor.
"In peace and silence you grow."

Nisargadatta Maharaj

Just in case you are feeling sad because things have changed at our house, nothing ever changes, not really. Just this morning the Swami-meister and I were going a few rounds. It began innocently enough. "Swami, don't you think we should think long and hard before we let just anyone come to your satsangs?" I said.

He screwed up his face as if he were lost in thought and said, "Judgment be damned. Full speed ahead." That afternoon six new people came and Swami had to experience the grace of the Self with a random assortment of nut cases (at least that is how they seemed to me). Some wanted grace, some wanted cookies and two wanted to know if he believed in reincarnation. "Sure do," snapped Swami. "There are too many jackasses around not to believe in it." I need to up his dosage of antacids.

The satsangs were getting to him; that much I knew. He is not the type to snap rudely at people, but people take their stupid pills before they come. They take their seats and wave good-bye to their brains. Not that enlightenment is mental, but one must at least show respect to the guru. I encouraged silence as the people came in and took their seats. The big hair people are asked to sit in the back and chewing gum is a no-no.

Sam raised his hand and asked Swami if there was any value in observing silence regularly. I knew that was the basis of his teachings. We moved in a sea of silence punctuated by our little crafts of sea-going words. Swami's words were usually only

indicators; nothing more. His finger had been pointing at the moon for so long that it was gnarled. "So, Sam," he said now, with a little weariness, "what's your real question?"

Of course Sam was nonplussed. Wasn't that his real question? Of course not; Swami knew that. He really wanted to know if Swami knew all about him and loved him anyway. Sam never came up with an answer, but Swami made sure that he "got it." How he did this I will never know; it is beyond me.

The Sixty-Four Dollar Question

"All this love is making me sick."

Swami Z

There is a sixty-four dollar question that Swami is able to answer better than anyone I have ever met. The question is always and only this: "Does God love me?" Swami dispenses love as he breathes it in and out. He wafts it in waves all around you. He is just an activator of your inner teacher. You dial him up and get your own thing going. Without leaving you arrive.

Sometimes, though, he just looks like a little old man you would see at the market. To see him push a grocery cart around is hilarious. He steers it into fat rumps and skinny legs. If you ever spot him there, run for your life. When he reaches the checkout counter, he's apt to have bought butter, bread, and banana peppers topped off with cream cheese, Cheese Whiz and Cheese Doodles. He favors soft toilet tissue and plenty of paper towels in the kitchen. Cookie-making is a messy thing. I swear we have sugar rings in the bathtub.

"Swami," I hollered at him as he was about to go out the kitchen door, "remember, satsang is at 3:00." Swami groaned. "All this love is making me sick." Lately the love vibes are becoming stronger and stronger. People who never heard of Swami now go around quoting him. I can't stand this. Swami has yet to say the first quotable thing. I know that for a fact. I am the one who follows him around as he says things like "Snuff, mrpghh and galrumph." Even this translates into love. One woman writes his word of the day on a sticky pad and reads it at regular intervals. It wouldn't be so bad except she reports back to the satsang and we have to listen.

"Swamiji said: Be kind." Here she squinted at the yellow sticky

note and pronounced slowly and triumphantly, "Be kind—derzma!" We all knelt at his feet intoning "Derzma!" Poor Swami. He got up and went to the kitchen, returning with some good hot prasad to distribute. Derzma indeed!

Heartthrob

"Swami, put your feet up and rest today," I said gently to him that afternoon.

"Ah, Vicki, I think I will. I need to fall back and regroup," was his reply. He looked tired.

"You're no spring chicken," I said to him, patting the top of his head.

"The satsangs are going extremely well," he said, going to the counter to put his mug in the sink.

"Just shows to go you that the heart knows what is best. I have to thank you for that, Vicki."

I looked at Swami in surprise. He was thanking me? Impossible. I had seen his wonder-working up close and personal for a couple of weeks now. People entered our little home looking frazzled and fussy. They left carrying homemade cookies and looking like angels.

What was he doing to these people? It was no use asking him, because he would just mumble something dumb. Believe it or not, I, too was succumbing to the "Swami said" tendency. When I went to the market and found myself in line behind an irate customer, I said to myself inwardly, "Swami says, 'No problem. Read some magazines. Pick out a new flavor of gum—whatever.'"

Swami ambled on down the hall to his room and I began unloading the cabinets so that I could wash them and put in new shelf paper. Something crossed my mind like a shadow. What if Swami got so popular that he left me? What would I do then?

My abandonment issues were alive and well. Swami popped his head around the corner and winked at me. He said three little words, "Not to worry." I pulled him into the kitchen and enveloped him in a hug. I would have done the dance of joy, but Swami was gone before I could begin. He might be a little senile at times, but he is clearly still a heartthrob.

The Guru Walk of Fame

Swami is getting a star on The Guru Walk of Fame. To that end, he has rented a tuxedo and I have sprung for a long, slinky red gown. We are somethin'! Swami doesn't look a day over 50 and me, well—let's just say I look terrif! If I hadn't pushed Swami into having satsang, we would not have been having this studly event for him. This is how it happened.

One fine day a limo pulled up in front of our modest home. Out hops an up-and-coming Hollywood starlet. She was draped on the arm of a movie mogul. Seems she got wind of Swami Z when she was in our little town making a low-budget movie. Swami was an extra on the day they needed "small, unassuming men." He fit the part, Lord knows.

I seated the two of them for satsang and she asked a leading question, "Does God exist or are we making him up?" I winked broadly at Swami, hoping that he would put her in her place. He didn't. Not only that, he was positively smitten. He did a tiny little dance of joy that you could hardly see and said, "Now, that's a fine question!"

He just stood there looking stupid. I finally cleared my throat until he came out of his reverie. "Are we making God up?" he repeated the question as if in a trance. Then he said loudly, "Well, what if we are?" There was a brief silence and then people began to clap. His performance was Oscar-worthy. "What if we are!" He said it as if it were a pronouncement for the ages. People looked downright happy, as if they had been bitten by the "What If We Are" bug. Darned if they hadn't been snookered by the best.

Love conquers all, however. I am loathe to admit this, but when said starlet called and said she wanted to put Swami on The Guru

Walk of Fame, I heartily agreed. I also knew that I didn't want him wearing his Dr. Scholl's sandals. But one thing at a time.

Gone Hollywood

Swami has gone Hollywood. He is now calling the satsang attendees his "peeps." And I don't mean Easter chickens. To make it worse, Rose is going along with it and encouraging him to do lunch and take meetings. Ruin has to take a number and Jim has been counseled to "lose the polyester." If it gets any worse, I may have to eliminate satsang altogether.

I am afraid he may speak to Entertainment Tonight about my housekeeping habits. Not only that, he will have them falling in love with my dust bunnies and feeding them carrots. I would jerk a knot in his tail, but he is running around the house jabbering. He's playing air guitar and chatting up Neil Young. I am in a quandary, a snit, and all points in between. I am so mad at him I am serving canned soup for supper. That will show him. Mister Big Shot the Guru. When did he ever enlighten anyone?

Prayerful

Swami and I have a prayer together every morning. It is for our own centering that we pray. Swami feels that being off-center is a bigger sin than almost anything else. He insists that we sit on folding chairs with our backs straight and our heads bowed. We let our hands hang loose in our laps.

Silence is the centering mechanism for both of us. It is like putting a level on a crooked picture. The silence levels the inner life right up because what is off-bubble is screaming for your attention. It feels like a brown shoe in a white shoe world. We look at the brown shoe and with focused energy on it, we breathe it out and let it go. We continue breathing until there are only white shoes left. Don't take this too literally since Swami usually wears slippers.

As we sit in silence together, I feel the love that Swami exudes with every breath he takes. This tiny man has the biggest heart of anyone I know. How I drew him to me is the biggest mystery of all. The silence extends into the other rooms of the house. Our bedrooms, the hall, kitchen and living room are touched by the soundlessness arising from within our hearts. My heart is not as big as Swami's, but it is beating in harmony with his. That gives me hope and the knowledge that for everything there is a season.

Swami's silliness over celebrity is just another game for the old man. He knows how radically all who love him are changed. It is nothing that he does, of course. You know this, by now. It is what he is that changes people. When we stand up, we hear our bodies creaking. Swami is the first to break the silence. "Well, Vicki," he says with vim, vigor and vitality, "let's eat!" I head for the kitchen, knowing that the cinnamon rolls are begging to be buttered. I can hardly wait.

P.S. For those of you who don't know or keep forgetting, Swami is a fictional character and I take no responsibility for what he does when I am off duty. If he gets under your skin or into your heart, don't tell me—tell him. Talk about a guru throwing you back on yourself.

Opening the Door

Swami has been asked this question before and perhaps now is as good a time as any to answer it. The question is this, "Why did you pick Vicki?" Swami thinks for a split second before breaking into a wide-mouthed jug of a grin. "Because she opened the door!" He pronounced this with all the energy of a three-year-old who has reached the top of a tree. "Vicki opened the door to a scrawny little man she had never laid eyes on before. Without hesitation, she let me into her heart and things started cooking." He continued, "I came to look after her. I make her cookies!"

Swami's Grace

Swami has not changed one iota since he moved in with me. He still bakes at odd hours, dresses funny, and is imperiously outspoken. What is it about this little guy that defies indifference? After all, he's a made-up dude. It's because truth is meant to be a consuming fire and that is exactly what he is. He loves unequivocally and with no apology. He deals truth like a gambler in Las Vegas and the odds are against your winning. He has you hook, line, and sinker. As Ramesh Balsekar said, "Your head is in the tiger's mouth." Grrrr.

Those who are open to Swami's teachings feel the unmistakeable love that he has for them. He doesn't just give it out in dribs and drabs; he slathers it on and turns the oven to 400 degrees. He wants you nice and roasted.

Skillfully, he peels away your facade and leaves himself nothing but the essence of you to be loved, loved, loved. Then he stands back and says proudly, "Look, what a loving disciple I have baked." He has thrown the scraps of your ego away and left the world with the best you that you could be. He should be on the Iron Chef. Alas, he is only a cookie maker.

The Truth is Neither Here Nor There

"The truth is what you make it and so are cookies."

Swami Z

Swami's satsang crowd is eating well these days—whether or not they are absorbing the truth is another matter. I imagine that their collective cholesterol count is staggering. Today the topic was about spontaneity. Swami gave a brief talk about hanging loose. He wore a Hawaiian shirt and flip-flops to drive his point home. Rose raised her hand with a question and sadly, it was key to everything. I say sadly because she never got it answered. It happened like this....

Rose put her pocketbook down and whipped out her notepad and pen. She was about to take Swami on. Little did she know how he worked. She tried to pin Swami down about being spontaneous and he was able deftly to avoid each question as it fell from pursed lips. Each time she raised a point, Swami parried and thrust until she was exhausted. I rarely saw Swami mad, but believe me, Rose was testing his patience.

"So, Swami," she ended up as if she were a skilled lawyer wrapping up her case, "hanging loose is something that you recommend?" Swami sat there picking at a thread on his lime green shirt. He finished and looked up at the ceiling.

"I have to follow the rules when I bake," Swami said. "Even though I can improvise on the recipes, I have to follow the rules when it comes to temperature and all that. The thing is, the cookies taste better when I make them in a surrendered state of mind."

Rose frowned. Clearly she was not comfortable with spontaneity, truth, and Hawaiian shirts. Did Swami care? I looked at him as

he arose and went to put an arm around Rose. I think I heard her inviting him over for pot roast. I looked around and everyone had gone back to their own reality. I was left with Swami and a roomful of empty chairs.

Slice and Bake Enlightenment

"Sleep fast. We need the pillows."
Old Yiddish Proverb

Swami began satsang with a statement, "I am here and you are there. Or to put it another way, you are here and I am there. Now that I have established that, it gets very confusing, for you often believe that you are other than here. When you think that you are here, it is then that you want to be there. And when you are there, it is then that you want to be here." Rose looked bored if not irritated. She raised her hand. "Yes, Rose, what is it?" said Swami.

"Why is it that you always end up acting silly? I know that I am here and you are there; do you have to act so silly about it?"

Swami said grumpily, "So, Rose, you are free to leave here and go there." Rose was a Type A; she just had to be accomplishing something. She went at understanding Swami like a bat out of hell. She was bent on taking him literally and at full throttle. Damn the torpedoes, full speed ahead. Swami was having none of it.

"Once when I was younger," said Swami, "I, too, pursued realization like it was the bullet train and I had just missed it. I put down my briefcase and ran like the devil. I finally caught it and it took me nowhere but there. It didn't stop here."

"Well, Swami, I have had quite enough of your stupid 'heres and theres'. I've heard of a better spiritual teacher that gives satsang quicker and faster."

"Yeah, slice and bake enlightenment. Doesn't taste so good, Rose. Got an artificial something or other—can't quite put my

94

finger on it," was his reply. He reached over and handed Rose a chocolate chip cookie. She took it and ended up eating the whole thing. By then, all of us were on Swami's side except Rose. Had she just come here for the cookies?

It's Not About the Cookies

Truth is stunningly simple. Take it or leave it; it remains. Bend it and twist it; it returns to its original shape. What is so complicated about this? Truth is above the human mind and emotions. It lies beyond our reach—on the top shelf. It is safe from our mishandling.

Truth would have us come to it on its terms and not on our own. Why is this so hard? Truth wants to free us from complexity; why is this beyond our grasp? Because it's supposed to be. Grasping is not how we come to truth.

Swami Z teaches little classes and people do not want to listen. He doesn't care; he knows what he's about. Forget complexity and come to class. It is not about the cookies. Or is it?

The Price of Admission

Swami Z sat behind his desk and waited for the few students that he had to settle down. He was obviously tired of this satsang business. He tried to jazz things up, but no one was buying it. "Stodgy old students," he thought, "wanting me to give them enlightenment so they can go out and brag about it."

Just last week the meter man had been in the side yard and Swami Z had asked him in for tea and cookies. He asked Swami no questions but he got infinity right there in our little kitchen. Imagine that.

Saturday Night

Saturday night was just like old times with Swami and me before he began giving satsang. We sat in the living room in front of the fire. Although spring was obviously in the offing, tonight was nippy and we drank cocoa and stared into the flames. I remembered the early days when Swami first came to live with me—how we fought and knocked heads and I loved every minute of it. Discipline has evolved gradually as I have come to respect him more as time goes by.

Of course, time doesn't go by; it just seems that way. Swami looked unusually peaceful and I had nothing to say to him that counted. I watched his abdomen rise and fall as he breathed. The fire crackled and I sighed deeply. If this was the simple life, I had achieved it. No, wait a minute. That doesn't sound right. Perhaps Swami had achieved it. But what was "it" and who was "I" to possess it? Swami was having his effect on the students who came to hang out with him in the satsang room. They knew nothing of his personal life and they didn't have to.

What they wanted and needed was his being and that was extraordinary. It transcended age, sex, and political opinions. It was rooted in the reality of being ordinary. As far as I know, Swami was affiliated with nothing—which is everything. The evening drew to a close and we each knew that all was well. Tomorrow, satsang would be held again and those who came would benefit from this evening. They would sit and listen to him speak, absorbing the atmosphere of this simple holy man. Cookies be darned; he alone was worth the price of admission.

The Game

Swami has been hanging out at Macy's again. I hate to tell you this, but having satsang at home has only increased his reputation with the ladies. They can't get enough of a Swami with a 350 thread count and a large Sharpie. Go figure. They meet him at Macy's and if he likes them, he invites them to our house for satsang. Sometimes, women argue over which folding chair affords the better view of Swami. Whether they are after his power or his money is beyond me. He looks after each devotee in whatever way their karma demands.

He offers Rose prasad of pimento cheese sandwiches with the crust cut off. For Jim, it's creamed tuna on toast. Needless to say, I have to wash up after these fatsos have gone. I am running low on pot scrubbers and elbow grease. Swami has little time to bake cookies, what with pot roast for Larry and twice-baked potatoes for Sam. The thing is—and I hope you don't think I am complaining—these satsangs are getting expensive. No one ever offers to wash dishes, either.

Today Larry wanted Swami to explain how grace trumps karma. I felt like getting out the poker chips and some cold ones. Swami had the perfect answer, though. He said that hearts beat grace. That went right over Larry's head. Last night I was so tired I was falling head first into the dishwater. Swami sat at the kitchen table swigging hot tea and holding his poor little head. "Got a headache?" I asked him.

He nodded wearily. "It's Larry's headache. He gave it to me when he told me good-bye—that sly little devil. If it isn't gone by morning, I'm giving it back and raising him a neck ache." Even Swami can be pushed too hard at times.

Initiation into Now

Swami entered the satsang room with an air of importance. He took his seat behind the desk and surveyed his listeners—all six of them. "Today," he intoned, "I am going to initiate you into now." He waited for a response. All he got was a dull thud. Rose had dropped her pocketbook. After she retrieved it and we were all satisfied that nothing else was going to happen, Swami went on.

"Now has everything that you need—like Rose's pocketbook." He ventured a half-smile, one of which Thich Nhat Hanh would have approved. "In the now is what you need to get through the day. And it may seem to last forever." He looked at his watch. "Sometimes today lasts well into tomorrow." He sighed and looked out the window. "Maybe it just seems that way when I have satsang with you people."

"You people" were not about to get their feet wet in the living moment, even with Swami nudging them into it. Rose took out a roll of candy and peeled one off and popped it into her mouth. She passed it to the person next to her in a conspiratorial fashion. She thought she was at the movies. I winced for what would come next.

Swami made one more stab at his not-so-gentle initiation into now. He rose suddenly, causing Rose to swallow her candy. I hoped someone knew the Heimlich maneuver, because Swami had left the building. He probably wanted to get a breath of fresh "now." I couldn't blame him.

I stayed long enough to see that the candy was dislodged, thanks to Myra's Heimliching of Rose—and then I passed out the cookies that were in the prasad basket. No one seemed to have noticed that Swami had disappeared. Is that what happened to

now? It just left unnoticed, only to be replaced by something more exciting? We were in big trouble. Swami's presence had not even been missed. Out in the yard he was giving satsang to the big oak tree—or was it the other way around?

Nuisance

Larry was becoming a nuisance. Not being known for nuances, he telegraphed his stupidity long before he had to. For instance, if I found myself humming music from the 80s, Larry would soon be making an appearance. I guess it's like people with migraines having auras beforehand. Larry has one, too. I can be well on my way to nirvana and *wham!* Larry, right in the old storyline. Here he comes now.

I heard a knock at the door. I knew it was Larry. He always uses the shave and a haircut knock. I let him in, albeit grudgingly. He was early for satsang, expecting cookies before class. What a dolt. Of course, I had conjured him up at a weak moment long before I had met Swami. Little did I know that Swami knew all about him. Larry sits in the back row so he can watch the door. When Swami is at full tilt, discussing samadhi, nirvana, and the bliss of the Self, Larry is apt to raise his paw.

"Got a question," said Larry, this Monday morning. "Do you believe that we choose our destiny?" Swami looked blank. He pulled at a thread on his plaid shirt. (He and Larry both favored plaid, I hate to admit this.) "Don't know and don't care," said Swami. "Got to deal with what is. That is destiny."

Larry couldn't leave well enough alone. He raised his hand a second time. This time Swami looked stern and let Larry wave his hand like a second-grader before he bit off the words, "Yes, Larry."

"What if you don't like what is?" he said.

"It probably doesn't like you, either," said Swami as if he knew something. "What say we move along?" But he had lost the class. They were busy hating Larry. I knew where they were coming from.

Above the Opposites

"Be of good hope in the face of death. Believe in this one truth for certain, that no evil can befall a good man either in life or death, and that his fate is not a matter of indifference to the gods."

Socrates

Larry never meant to cause any trouble. The Larrys of this world never do. They are born *in utero* with swamis and persist until full enlightenment. I don't know this, for I am making it up like everything else. There is a good twin and an evil twin. I had no idea that Larry would be poking his ugly old head in at satsang and keeping me up nights. No idea....

Swami loves Larry even though he is a giant aggravation. He beams at Larry just as he beams at poor, hapless Rose. Today Rose had a sardine sandwich in her bottomless handbag. Swami would be right in the middle of saying something that was key to waking up and would then get a whiff of sardines.

"Listen up, you people," said Swami stentoriously. "Every day is the last day—it could be—" sniff, sniff. "What the heck is that awful smell?" Rose said nothing. Swami continued, trying not to gag. "Death is here now; just as life with a small 'l'. Life is above the opposites—what the heck is stinking up satsang?"

Rose finally admitted guilt and was not forgiven until she had passed the sandwich around and let us all sniff indignantly. She ate it in full waking consciousness in the presence of life and death. Satsang over.

Stick Pony Drill

This morning I heard a knock at the door. When I opened it, there stood Larry holding Ruin, his stick pony. "Vicki," he said with his usual hubris, "I want to start a stick pony drill team."

"I don't own a stick pony," I said (with profound relief).

"Oh, I know you don't. That'll come later. For now, just use a broom. I want us to learn how to march together. We're meeting at Starbucks. Here's a good idea—maybe we can call ourselves the Starbuckeroos." He looked inordinately proud of himself. He was wearing a white cowboy hat and a plaid polyester shirt.

"Larry," I improvised, meanwhile sending up a prayer to heaven, "let me think about it. I have a lot of things to do today. I have to do my taxes and soak my head." I knew he wasn't listening and he proved it by total non-reaction to the head soaking comment. He just unhitched Ruin from my mailbox and rode off into the sunset, which was hard since it was before noon. Later I saw him at Dunkin' Donuts eating coconut cake donuts and drinking coffee from a paper cup.

A Rhetorical Question

"Swami," I said as I lay on the floor in front of the fireplace, "what do you think about stopping satsang. I mean—no one is even close to getting it."

"So," said Swami with an unusually provocative inflection. "Have you gotten it?"

That is what you call a rhetorical question since he obviously knew the answer. Why he stayed on here was beyond me. I was so rooted and grounded in his love that I took it for granted these days. He was a frail old man who forgot things. "If he left you for good," said my mind, "what would you do?"

I hoped that Swami was not reading my thoughts. He must not have been, for he looked up and said the following, "Beloved Vicki, who took me in and gave me use of her stove, I have no intention of stopping satsang. Anyone who comes here is free to take what I have to give—and eat cookies while I am giving it."

Thanks to Swami, the Girl Scouts no longer sold as many boxes of cookies on our street. They couldn't top Swami's.

"Satsnag"

Yesterday Larry had been at satsang again. He had the nerve to ask a question with a toothpick hanging out of his mouth. "Swams," he said, dropping the "i" in a familiar way, "once we get it, can we keep it?"

"Of course you can, Larry," said Swami generously, "and I shall give you a paper bag to carry it home in." Rose tittered. She was actually coming along nicely. Never underestimate the power of a woman who uses breath mints on the hour. She is apt to be meticulous in the dharma as well.

"Rose," said Swami patiently, "would you please tell us what it is that I am trying to give you?"

"Satsang,"said Rose simply.

I would have thought she was just another ditsy old broad, but who knows? She was definitely ahead of Larry.

It's in the Script

Some days, satsang never gets off the ground. We are only human, including Swami Z. Today was one of those days your mama told you about. Swami was wearing a shirt that made him itch; Rose had a cough and I was just generally morose. I wanted Swami back all to myself. These wannabe *chelas* were getting on my nerves. I was overeating and whining to Swami about it every chance I got.

It was a beautiful day. Why were we so contrary and unappreciative of the world's cutest swami? He sat there with his hand at the back of his neck looking like a five-year-old. I couldn't remember if I had any calamine lotion or not. If I did, I would make him put some on. He talked about service to the guru and how important it was in purifying our hearts. (Was it because I was behind in doing his laundry?) "Vicki is the perfect disciple," I heard him saying. "She writes down everything I say." Well, now he was being ironic, bordering on sarcastic.

Larry chose that moment to ask if he could be excused. "Larry," said Swami sternly, "you should go to the bathroom before satsang begins." I squirmed. Larry sighed and slumped in his folding chair. Why did he keep coming to satsang?

If you are wondering why Swami and I put up with Larry, it is simple. He's in the script. The script is that thing we all have to follow whether we want to or not. Usually our lines are not ideal and we read them with far too much identification. Swami calls this "chewing the scenery instead of the cookies." Larry sulked during the rest of satsang. Rose went to sleep. John asked a stupid question and Swami just kept scratching. Thankfully, he aborted the whole satsang well before the usual time and we all exited stage left. Offstage I put calamine on Swami's neck and told myself repeatedly that he was just a piece of fiction. Love lies beyond the printed page.

Where We Are Joined to God

Today Jim raised his hand with a question about surrender. "How do I surrender when there is no one there?" he asked. I looked at him in his gray polyester pants and saw a gentle giant. There had been no one there in the negative sense for some time now. Jim was as serene as they come. In fact, if he was unsurrendered, I had only just begun. I was a weisenheimer in the company of the wise.

"Jim," said Swami, with the softest of half-smiles, "surrender happens. Look at Ruin; he doesn't worry about letting go of thought." Ah, we were back to Ruin again. We returned there frequently, as now Larry was allowing us to ride Ruin after satsang. It was a liberating experience to trot him around the back yard, letting him stop to eat grass. Sometimes I remembered the freedom of childhood. And at other times, I just rode him right into a tree. I am still a bit clumsy.

"Swami," I said, shuffling through a stack of coupons, "where do you think we are joined to God?"

"There is only one answer to such a stupid question," said Swami with an unusual air of sternness.

"Ya got me," I said, thinking of Sara Lee and Hershey Kisses, wondering what I would cook for dinner.

"You are one with God at the point where you are able to be honest with Him. You are with Him all of the time, but it doesn't do you any good until you stop lying."

"Who, me?" I said, knowing full well that Swami hated me being a smart aleck.

Priceless

Swami needs to see a shrink. He is going around acting like somebody just stepped on his last nerve. He is yelling at students to speak louder, say less, and yes, last week he was heard to say, "Bite me." Often Swami watches too much TV; hence the expressions "Bite me" and "Yada, yada, yada." Once he was expounding on the Gita and he just said "Yada, yada, yada." If it doesn't sound funny now, you just had to be there.

Swami has also taken to eating nachos and cheese dip. I am seriously concerned about this particular habit. If Larry sees Swami eating cheese dip, the next thing you know—Ruin is covered in it. Swami borrowed Ruin yesterday to ride to the Quick Mart. With his bed sheet blowing in the wind, he was a handsome sight, if I do say so. When they got home, he thanked Larry for the loan and apologized for letting Ruin have a Slurpee. Ruin now has a purple mouth and everyone in satsang wants to take him home and clean him up.

Satsang attendees are learning how to do chores around our house. Before class, some of them troop into the kitchen and dust baseboards—things like that. Jim sprayed the house for roaches last week and Rose dusted us all down with lavender sachet. Cleanliness is next to godliness and smelling "purty"— well, that's priceless.

Snit

I have been in a snit lately. You see, everybody loves Swami and no one gives a fig about me. When Swami came to live with me, I was oh, so generous with the little Napoleonic figure. I let him wear my bed sheets; I washed up after his cookie messes and let him have the run of the house.

He would sweep out the door on his way to Macy's, come home and sit down to my delicious dinners and fall asleep in front of the fire or the TV. I was Cinderella by my own hearth. I took it all in stride. But since Swami started holding satsang, I've become a wee bit resentful. He knows it and is playing me like a fiddle.

"Vicki's mad and I am glad and I know what will please her. A bottle of ink to make her stink and Swami Z to squeeze her." He danced around me wildly and I was tempted to pull the plug on my computer. It would be that easy. Rose, Jim, Larry—all the attendees would just up and disappear. No more cookies, no more Swami. Ah, I was contemplating the power when Swami stepped on my foot.

"You just stepped on my last nerve!" I yelled. Swami looked gratified and horrified at the same time. I began to cry and like all little boys, Swami didn't know what to do. He stood there transfixed as tears rolled down my face. Finally he gave me a hug and said, "I'm sorry. I promise to let you watch anything you want on TV tonight." He went into the kitchen and put the kettle on. And here I am at the computer, begging for your love, just as I might be on American Idol. Only I am old enough to know better.

A Gold Mine

"Paradise is always where love dwells."

Richter

Swami sat with a newspaper underneath his feet clipping his toenails. "Swami!" I yelled. "Stop it! I will not write you any further into this piece until you stop." Swami calmly completed his left foot, folded the paper, and put it in the wastebasket. Again I yelled. "For the love of Mike!" He was hopeless. But I began typing and we went on from there. You may think it is odd that Swami has life both as a character and when he is not. But this is no different than how people behave. In fact, it is exactly how they behave. Swami, of course, knows that he is just a dream that I am having. "Look out the window," said Swami. "Here come Michael, Rose, and Jim. They are all just stick figures to me."

"Then where does the love you feel for them come from, Swami?" I asked.

"From within, of course, Vicki. It is time to fire up the satsang." He grabbed his glass of water and we entered the addition. We looked out over Swami's groupies and I sat down. Having a front row seat to Swami is "like buttah."

The topic was being real. Swami tended to be lazy about his satsangs and so he just pulled that topic to him because it was the closest. "None of us are real," said Swami, glancing over at me typing him into the computer. "Here's where it gets complicated." (One of Swami's favorite throwaway lines.) Rose scooped it up and put it in her purse.

"Just last night, I was baking cookies and someone knocked at the door. It was a reader from Kansas who just had to have

some of my cookies and receive my darshan. I said, 'As far as I know, we are fresh out of darshan.' I gave her some cookies and because she believes in me, she had no trouble digesting them. And she will never, ever, gain any weight!"

I hope WeightWatchers never gets a whiff of Swami or they will buy him, turn him into a product, and weigh his fat grams.

By now, the satsang attendees are thinking instead of listening. They are trying to figure out how they can come to satsang and lose weight at the same time. Can't be done—unless the fat isn't real, either. This satsang could turn out to be a gold mine.

A Giggle

Swami is a giggle. Even when he is lowering the boom, he comes across as warm. Go figure. The satsang attendees often come through the door looking glumly human—to put it nicely. Swami can take their weariness and dip it into a jar of bubble solution.

"What's that, Rose? You're feeling your age today?" Swami dips his awareness into the bubbles and blows good energy to Rose. Rose, being the perfect example of taking things literally, stands up and catches his energy, holding it gently on her palm. We all look at it with wonder, especially me, who is making this up as I go along. I stopped typing long enough to look at the bubbles in Rose's hand, then continued typing. Swami feigned exasperation, "Now, Rose, don't take everything I say so literally. Put my energy down and pay attention."

Rose sat up straighter in her chair. Larry came in late, propped Ruin against the wall and took a back seat. Swami feigned even more irritation. "Larry, you and that darned fool pony are late!"

Larry hung his head and Ruin looked unworried. After satsang was over, Swami gave Ruin some sugar cubes and Rose a hug. Beats me if anyone learned anything today.

The Essence of the Teachings

"Letting go will happen when it happens.
Until then it is just another eff-orting thought!"

Swami Z

I hope that none of you are taking Swami literally. That is to miss the essence of the teachings, which is your unreality. If Swami let her, Rose would climb into his lap and hand-feed him his lines. She always records what he says verbatim and that is verboten. Last week he was speaking and she asked him to repeat something that he said too fast. "Eh, er—uh—I was, uh...." said Swami. But he had lost the point. He made do with another point, but I don't remember what it was.

All of a sudden Swami roared, "What am I, a lightning bug? Am I something that you can catch, squash and wear as a ring?" Rose took this literally. Satsang ended with Rose chasing Swami around with a large butterfly net. She wanted his body, but not for the usual reasons.

Swami's Kindness

"Can you breathe in and out? Can you be kind?"

Lama Yeshe

Swami's kindness is beyond understanding. On a day when you think he is going to kick someone out of satsang, he lowers the bar so that someone like Larry can jump across. Larry had come in late, wagging Ruin along as usual. Swami had let it be known that he loved Ruin like a brother, which really confused us. Stick ponies are not generally that lovable.

Larry propped Ruin carefully by his chair and looked up at Swami. Swami said, with a hint of irritation, "Larry, I was right in the middle of transcending karma and you come in late. Now I have lost my train of thought."

Rose waggled her hand like a schoolgirl. "I remember," she said, "You were saying," (and here she consulted her notes) "that karma is something that rises and turns into...." she frowned. "Oh, that is my recipe for angel biscuits," she said. Swami smiled softly.

Wanting to be stern with Larry, though, he wiped the smile off and addressed Larry's lateness. "Larry, I can no longer put up with your coming to satsang late. You cannot attend tomorrow. You must remember that time is to be used for waking up. What if I ring the dharma bell and you are not here?"

Larry didn't seem to understand what Swami was getting at, and Swami, in his innate kindness, let the moment pass. After satsang, he reached down and patted Ruin gently on his little brown head. Anyone who owns a stick pony named Ruin can't be all bad.

More in Love

Jim raised his hand and tried to steer the conversation in another direction. "Swami, I had a near-life experience once. I was dating a girl and was right on the verge of asking her to marry me. I got cold feet—went right back to my usual life. I've been a bachelor for 15 years."

"There you have it," said Swami. "A case-study of the perfect near-life experience." Jim looked pleased to have been singled out and Swami pretended not to see. Instead he raised his head to look at the old oak tree. Swami might be squirrelly, but more importantly, he is really alive where it counts.

"Sometimes," said Swami, "life is not so much about what you make it as about what it makes of you." He said these words on a fine spring morning when the pear trees were bearing white shawls of blossoms on their slender shoulders. Swami looked very fine himself. Although he was an old man, he was wiry and electrically ecstatic. Where did he get this immediacy with all of life?

I raised my hand on an impulse. "Yes, Vicki?"

"Swami, who is the true guru? I know that the question itself is a cliche, but I still want to know."

"Your guru is the one who changes you in spite of yourself, the one who awakens love in you—the one who forces you to abandon all that is not love. In other words, the guru is everywhere."

Everyone in the satsang room was watching Swami intently. There was something different about his energy field today that was extraordinary. When he moved, he moved in a field of white light. The hairs on my neck were standing up.

"And if I am everywhere, then so are you. If I am love, then so are you. If I have power, then so do you." I swear that Jim would have given his power back if he could have. He squirmed in his folding chair. "Jim," said Swami, with precognitive insight, "keep your power." Jim said nothing, but when he rose to leave the satsang room, Swami walked over to him and gave a slight bow. "Thou art that, Jim," he said, "and all the tea in China won't take it back."

Now why did the rest of us fall even more deeply in love with Swami?

Witnessing the Chaos

If we can witness the chaos within without trying to interfere, it will die down of itself. This is one of the root truths of all spiritual teachings. Christ said, "Resist not evil," and many masters have restated this key principle. We resist receiving it.

Gurdjieff taught that, "Man cannot do." There are some who call his teachings coldly intellectual; however, they have stood the test of time. Just try and do anything about your pain and sorrow. You will find out how little power you have.

The silence of our inner self is a bulwark against the noise of life. Although ever-present, it must be entered with the wish to transcend the clamor of our everyday consciousness.

The Law of Levity

Swami is threatening to pull the plug on satsang. I keep telling him that we have a lot invested in the new addition to the house; he won't listen. Seems he is just sick and tired of people not changing. Yesterday a man named Solomon attended for the first time and thought he knew everything there was to know about the path. He was old and well-read. Unfortunately, he was emotionally childish. He kept interrupting Swami to raise questions. That has never gone over well with Swami.

The subject that Swami had chosen to speak about was suffering—about how we all suffer and think it is unique to us. We really don't give a fig about the sufferings of other people. "For instance," said Swami, "I am suffering in the moment because none of you are listening to me fully. You are too busy suffering. You think I have nothing new to say about the topic. You think you know better. You *think*—and that's the problem."

That day was a watershed day for both Swami and me and I can't figure out why. I only know that humor (the law of levity) was replaced by gravity and some people fell down and got hurt.

Gurus Are Out

Swami was nowhere to be seen in the satsang room. The chair behind his desk was empty. I watched the attendees file in and take their seats, a bit nervous about not seeing him up there as usual. I wasn't sure what to do. I had no protocol for this; nothing in my notes to prepare me. Of course, he gets cantankerous at times—even a bit testy—but he was flat gone! Rose, of course, was the first to speak. "Where's Swami, Vicki?"

"I have no idea, Rose," I said. "Surely he'll walk in at any minute." But he didn't. Jim and a couple of the men went out back to see if he was there. He was lying in the hammock sound asleep. All they heard was the familar "ZZZZZZ." Jim poked him gently on the shoulder a couple of times and Swami opened his eyes. "No satsang today," he said, rather sadly. "Gurus are out."

Larry had wandered into the backyard about that time. He parked Ruin by the hammock and said, "What do you mean, gurus are out?" Like he should care. Anyone who wears a mullet and rides a stick pony couldn't care less about the In and Out list of spiritual wannabes.

"Gurus are out," repeated Swami. "I read it somewhere. Anyway, all of you can go home. When gurus come back in, I'll let you know." Rose clasped her bosom in disbelief. "Let me know—let me know," she said with surprising indignity. "I may be dead by then!"

Swami got up out of the hammock with Larry's help and took time to stroke Ruin. "If gurus are out—well then, I'm so out I'm in."

"That's the ticket," said Jim, wiping his hands on his blue

polyester shirt. Come to think of it, not many people who came to Swami's satsang cared whether they were in or out about anything. Airstream trailers, polyester shirts, and crocheted tissue covers were held in high esteem by these spiritual students. It was one of those days that ended well. Swami gave a talk about loving what is and topped it off with double-chocolate chip cookies. Ruin loved being outdoors and frankly, so did the rest of us.

*Note to those who say gurus are not in. Get out! And Ruin had this to say, "Bite me!"

On Having No Head

There has been a terrible accident. Larry and Ruin were heading home after satsang. From what the police can tell us, a blue Ford Mustang rear-ended Larry. No one was hurt, but Ruin's head came off, leaving Larry only a stick to ride. Those of us who love Ruin were devastated. We weren't sure what to do. We couldn't send him get-well cards because he couldn't read. We couldn't send casseroles because his digestive system had been disconnected from his mouth.

How do you let a stick know that you love it? I thought about Douglas Harding's brilliant book, *On Having No Head*. I could visit Ruin and Larry and read aloud from it. I lost no time in finding the book and hightailing it over to Larry's. Larry lived in a trailer park. It was a lovely one with little Toto-like dogs waiting to be blown away. Red geraniums spilled from goose planters and wagon wheels were growing out of the dirt like fine landscaping materials.

Larry's trailer was an old Airstream. I knocked at the door and Larry let me in. He had obviously been crying. The accident had shaken him up, but more than that, his best friend lay in two parts on the sagging corduroy couch. Silently I approached the motionless horse. Tears were welling up in Larry's eyes as he said, "He's not long for this world."

I thought to myself that he wasn't long, period! He had never been more than two hands high and without his head, he was definitely a miniature pony. His head lay on one cushion and his body further on down the couch. I sat between the two Ruins and wished I had gone to veterinary school, or at the very least—to a doll hospital.

Larry said, "Guess he's not good for anything but the glue

factory." That was it! I asked Larry if he had some wood glue and he did. We operated on Ruin right away. Without rubber gloves or sterilization, we put Ruin's head and his body on the kitchen table and performed crude surgery. Re-attaching the head to the body was a risky procedure; we knew that. But, however dangerous it was, it had to be done. Otherwise, Ruin would have no quality of life at all—not to mention Larry.

Hours later, Larry and I came to. (We had fallen asleep after the re-attachment was complete.) We raced into the kitchen where Ruin still lay on the kitchen table. Would he be able to ride again? I put my hand on his neck and the glue held. I turned to Larry and said with emotion, "Would you like to ride him around the room—but carefully?"

Larry lifted Ruin off the table and took the reins in his hand. I, overcome with emotion, could only watch as they galloped around the green ottoman. It had all been worth it. I guess I wouldn't be reading from Douglas Harding after all!

PART III

The True Guru

"Maybe that's what life is—a wink of the eye
and winking stars."

Jack Kerouac

The True Guru

Swami has proclaimed Ruin to be the true guru. He now bows to Ruin whenever he sees him. Ruin, simple being that he is, never takes it into himself, but remains unperturbed. Today we held satsang in the garden, among the flowers and random weeds. Jim was eager to raise a question about the nature of reality.

"Swami," he asked earnestly, "am I real?" Swami turned to Ruin and gently inclined his head. "Is Ruin real?"

"Of course not," said Jim.

"Yet would you not say that Ruin is relatively real?" asked Swami. "To Larry, he is realer than real." Larry turned in Swami's direction. He had fallen asleep, truth to tell, and only roused himself when he heard Ruin's name. "Ruin—did you say Ruin? Where is he?" Larry has developed a deep fear of losing Ruin. We think it is an old abandonment issue, but he is in denial.

"We were saying that Ruin is real to you, is he not?" Larry beamed with pride as he looked toward the love of his life. "He is the real deal," replied Larry. "I'm going to put him up on eBay!" Oh, my God. Say it's not so. Is Larry this shallow, egotistical, and self-serving?

Swami blanched. "You can't mean this, Larry. You would sell the Self that you are? You would trade the Real for cash?"

"No," said Larry. "I am using PayPal."

I couldn't listen anymore. If Ruin can be bought and sold, maybe I can sell Swami for a song.

Larry and Ruin

Larry and Ruin have taken up yoga. It's not enough that Larry is attending satsang. Oh, no; now I have to write him into a yoga class. Until you've seen Larry salute the sun wearing chaps, you haven't lived. He rides Ruin to class and I jog along with them, wishing that I could ride Ruin myself. But Larry is selfish, as you all know. Lest you dislike Larry, let me hasten to remind you that he lets Ruin get in bed with him when it storms.

But I digress. Larry is going to yoga because I do. He has no inner sense of what's good for him. He eats Doritos for breakfast and forgets to brush his teeth. He lets his hair grow so long the mullet becomes as flat as a flounder and his pores are much too large. His nose is beaky and he wears boots at all times. Ruin, however, is a sleek wooden pony that rides like the wind. He knows that Larry needs him and yet he never throws this in his face. Even when Larry forgets to feed him, he is forgiving.

Today Larry is having trouble doing the lion. You have to stick your tongue out as far as you can and make a ferocious face. He can only look so ferocious. I glanced over at Ruin and saw his everlasting look of peace. His expression never changes. Ah, to be so enlightened.

Stick Pony Wisdom—Learning to Ride Like the Wind

"You have to go through Larry to get to Ruin."

Vicki

I wanted to see Ruin last week and Larry wouldn't let me. What happened was this. I had a very bad week, one in which the sky had fallen on me in sharp, jagged pieces. I was cut by cumulus and nicked by nimbus. Only Ruin could heal me. I stopped by the Airstream and knocked on the door. Larry answered. "What's up?" he said in his usual laconic manner.

"I want to take Ruin for a ride," I said, knowing full well that Larry seldom let Ruin go out alone. He claimed that Ruin needed him. What a joke. Larry clung to Ruin like a cheap suit. The only reason Ruin lived with him was that he was choiceless in the matter. If he'd had legs, he would've run away from Larry a long time ago.

No, that is not exactly true. I am just being bitter and self-serving. Ruin loves Larry and lives with him because it is the right thing to do. But I needed a stick pony to ride this morning. I sent up a silent prayer—that I could ride Ruin around the trailer park at the very least. I needed to feel the wind in my hair and the gravel under my tennies.

Larry gave in—on one condition. I had to take the two of them out to dinner. The All-You-Can-Eat fish fry. "Okay," I said. I took Ruin from the corner and spoke gently in his ear. The words were right from the heart and Ruin seemed to know just what I needed.

We galloped joyfully around Airstreams and geranium pots. I

waved at snaggle-toothed kids and old men sitting in worn lawn chairs. My head was beginning to clear and my wounds were beginning to heal. No wonder Larry liked to keep Ruin to himself. This was better than sex.

That night, as we plowed our way through catfish and hushpuppies, I knew the answer to the secret of life. But like Larry, I am loath to share.

Wind Horse

Ruin has run away. I have never seen Larry so upset. When I tried to get him to open up about it, he just turned his face to the wall. He was on his naugahyde couch at the time. "Larry, if you don't tell me what happened, how will I be able to find Ruin?" I said.

Larry looked frighteningly bad. His mullet clung to his head and his breath was fetid. There were empty Cheetos bags littering the floor. I persisted. "When did he run?"

"Last night. We came home from Walmart and I put him on the counter with the stuff I had bought. I meant to put him in the corner like I always do, but I forgot. When I came back, he was gone." I was deeply disturbed. What if Ruin had fallen into the hands of evil? Into the hands of someone who wouldn't cherish him like Larry did? Just yesterday they had attended satsang together. Swami had patted Ruin on his little brown head and received his darshan. I dreaded telling Swami.

I decided to look around the trailer, just in case Larry had overlooked a clue as to why Ruin would have run. It didn't take me long to solve the case of the missing stick. He was on the closet shelf where Larry kept his extra toilet paper. The toilet paper was in the corner where Ruin was usually tethered.

"Larry, Larry," I yelled. "It's okay. You got confused and put Ruin on the shelf."

Larry said, "Why would I do that?"

"It really doesn't matter," I sighed. "The important thing is that you still have Ruin. And enough toilet paper to last you for a month. Do you mind if I borrow a few rolls?"

Larry didn't hear me. He was doing things to Ruin that embarrassed me to see. He was kissing him in the mouth and Ruin looked positively panicked. I hoped he didn't try to run tonight. There's always a first time for everything.

Two Left Feet

Swami Z has two left feet. I know because he has been dancing around the house, touched by the spring warmth. Flowering trees are in bloom and Swami is growing younger. He has the radio on and is jammin', but not very gracefully. I don't think he knows the difference between his two feet. Ah, well....

Today in satsang we had a quiet, rather boring group. Larry came late, sat in the back row and chewed Juicy Fruit. His mullet was oily and his plaid shirt was downright ugly. I was embarrassed for him. And wouldn't you know it, he raised his hand. When Swami called on him, this is what he said—more or less. "Swami, is Vicki going to be enlightened or should she just pack it up now? I mean, she has been hanging around you for a loooong time."

The clock ticked loudly while Larry waited for his answer. Finally Swami started singing "Get on the love train—dah dah dah—get on the love train—dah dah dah." I winced, Larry left and the disciples danced. A good time was had by all.

Through "Think and Then"

The next satsang featured singing birds, as we all trooped outside on a beautiful warm afternoon. Swami sat on a bench connected to the picnic table and the others were in lawn chairs. A pitcher of lemonade and a plate of cookies awaited us. Swami seemed bent on continuing the theme of the true guru. He lobbed this comment into the small crowd, "Is the true guru going to stay with you through think and then...." Swami loved word play as much as I did.

"Do you mean through thick and thin?" said Rose, ever the literal-minded.

"No, I meant through think and then," said Swami, beginning to get irked with Rose.

"Thinking about God won't cut the mustard," said Swami. "Talking about Him isn't much better. Being God, now that's the ticket!" he proclaimed. Jim, of course, turned beet-red and slumped down in his chair.

"Swami Jim," said Swami loudly, "what is the nature of reality? Be real!" thundered Swami, rising up off the wooden bench. "Be a man!" Right then, as if on cue, a squirrel ran down the tree and scampered into the yard. We all looked at it, as if it might somehow rescue Jim.

"You know why you can't respond, Jim?" asked Swami. "Because you are too modest to be God. If I needed God in you, you wouldn't be able to summon Him. How about you, Rose, got God today?"

Rose clutched her handbag defensively. "What?" was all she could manage to say. I was growing protective of the other

disciples. Swami was being unfair. No one can summon God on cue. Didn't Swami know that? A silence fell over the satsang assembled in the backyard. Who would be able to segue into another subject? We didn't have to wait long to find out. Swami stood up and said that satsang was over for today. He passed among us with the plate of cookies and everyone took at least two. I'm not sure that counts as being hungry for God, but who knows?

An Appetite for Satsang

Last night Swami and I sat at the kitchen table and talked about satsang. More and more people were flocking to hear Swami speak. It doesn't matter what he says; what matters is that he says it. He cannot help but help; it's his nature. Of course, as his student, I find myself growing more and more morose. That is my nature.

"I'm down in the dumps," I said, hoping for a hug or just the right combination of words, like pepperonis placed on a pizza.

"You!" said Swami, with disbelief. "I'm the one selling river water at the river. I'm getting downright wet." He shook his head as he licked the spatula and walked it to the sink. Plunging it under hot running water, he continued his diatribe. "Jim wants his enlightenment at a steady 70 degrees and Rose—well, Rose has no earthly idea about any of it. She has a full purse and an empty brain and she is *not* about to give either one up."

"What about Larry?" I said timidly. "Don't you think Larry is making progress?"

"Larry is Larry. While I wish him well, Ruin will realize himself before Larry. By the way, I see that the sale of stick ponies is up since you've been writing about Ruin. Makes me want to get one myself."

"Now, Swami," I said, standing up and pushing back from the table. "That horse won't hunt. Let's have some tea and turn on TV." That night I dreamt I was riding Ruin across the range. Larry and Swami were running along behind me in hot pursuit. I had made off with an entire batch of chocolate chip cookies. When I woke up, I was starving.

Inside Out and Upside Down

I am wondering why anyone bothers to attend satsang anymore. It is turning out to be inside out and upside down. Swami is making Jim read excerpts from Gurdjieff's *All and Everything* and Larry has to—get this—read the recipes in Rose's recipe box aloud. Swami commandeered it last month and Rose was stupidly happy to let him borrow it. So now we are up to our eyeballs in The Work and ground beef. Go figure.

Gurdjieff and Rose are not compatible; leastwise I don't think so. The whole kit and caboodle of us are undergoing conscious suffering on a mass basis. While we're not many in number, our bodies are heavy-weights. As far as understanding the words of Mr. G., I had rather make a cassoulet blindfolded.

Today Larry is reading from "Meatball Stroganoff" and Jim is deep into "Mr. G." I would quote that for you, but hey, get it off the Internet. It is complex enough out in the backyard; I don't want to have to transcribe it for your reading pleasure. It might be good with more sour cream; I have no idea. The Work and the recipes are both time-consuming and altogether frustrating. I am used to Swami doing the cooking.

Larry favors peanut butter and has no idea why he has been chosen to read recipes. He is admitting (finally) to being obsessed with Ruin. We adore Ruin and this makes for complicated issues, for you can't have one without the other. Rose had Ruin for the weekend and returned him in better shape than he had been in for years. She fed him dog biscuits and rubbed him down with lanolin. He loved the attention.

But back to the reading of Gurdjieff and the recipe cards. While Rose's recipes are loaded with calories, "Mr. G" is loaded with unpronounceable words. Jim is becoming both fat and

tongue-tied. Swami loves to create confusion and so he is in his element. He stated with religious fervor that food is meant to be eaten first in the mind's eye and that Mr. G. was the best he had ever tasted. It is time for me to remind you, the reader, that Swami is senile and that I am running out of ideas for this satsang. Y'all come back now, ya hear?

Frustration

"All you people want from me are words and cookies," Swami said. He looked genuinely sad. Could it be possible that we were using him up like a box of tissues and that one day he would be empty? Swami shook his head as if to clear it and then said, "You people are wordly. I don't mean worldly. I mean wordly. What have I ever said to you that changed you?" We just sat there.

"Anybody?" he said with an air of unfeigned sorrow. "I'm taking my words back. I can put them to better use somewhere else." He meant it. He didn't really take his words back; he just forced us to listen to the meaning behind the silence that he gave us instead.

When the silent satsang ended, we played around in the kitchen like children who had not yet learned to talk. We ate cookies and smiled warmly at each other. Larry spoke the words that broke the silence, but I don't remember what they were. Just as well.

That night the old house sat containing two people with nothing but silence between them. Swami and I were embodying the Self like we were going out of style—and we were. People these days are looking for the quick fix, like instant pudding. Swami's wisdom is assimilated slowly—sipped rather than gulped. Most of his "regulars" realize this. They were destined to learn from the master and are choiceless in the matter. Others come and go like so many fads.

Whoever turns to truth for consolation generally doesn't find it. Consolation is available on the human level, but not on the spiritual one. On the higher level, self-disappearance is the only consolation given.

Just a Piece of Fiction

I sat in the kitchen feeling every nerve. Swami was mixing up a batch of dough and I watched him with irritation. Suddenly he turned and said, "Vicki, you are making me jumpy. What are you thinking?" I heaved a sigh. What had I been thinking? It had already slipped away. Something about disappointment that I had not been given a better, more worthy guru. I know, I know. Swami is beloved to many of you by now. To me he has become just a piece of fiction.

His clear brown eyes never looked any older to me. Right now they settled on my inner being and wouldn't let go. He wanted my full attention. After he had put the cookies in the oven and set the timer, he came and sat with me. Taking my hands in his two clean ones, he said, "Tell me what you were thinking."

"That I wanted a more powerful teacher, a more exalted life than the one I have been given. Sitting here in the kitchen with you is a drag." He looked pained. Suddenly I felt Swami rather than saw him. He was sorrowful. Shocked by this new awareness, I said nothing. The clock ticked loudly and the cookies scented the air.

"You always get the teacher you deserve—and the grace you have earned."

"I thought grace wasn't earned," I whined.

"Paradox, Vicki, think paradox. Can't you lift your life above your feelings and see it?"

What I saw was Swami. What I felt was sorrow. Was this all there would ever be? The timer buzzed so loudly that I jumped. Swami obediently turned it off and took the cookie sheet from the

oven. His newest batch was butterscotch chip. As depressed as I was, I ate three before they cooled off. I sighed as I washed up the bowls and utensils. Swami had gone outside to sit in the swing. I had let him down.

The next thing I knew I heard laughter. Larry and Ruin had come over. Ruin was propped against the lawn swing and Larry and Swami were having a light-hearted conversation. I was jealous. Should I join them or just go to my room? This bit of a karmic dilemma was resolved a little later. Swami poked his head into the living room and said, "Vicki, Larry is here and wants you to join us." I walked into the backyard to find Larry, Ruin, and Swami playing croquet. Larry was using Ruin for his mallet and suddenly I didn't feel so stupid.

Hunger

Swami looked into the pantry, saying that he was hungry. "How could you be hungry?" I asked in disbelief. He had just eaten a breast of chicken, mashed potatoes, two biscuits, and some green beans. "I want—I want—some...." He trailed off miserably. This was not like the Swami I knew. He walked around the room like a tiger pacing. He glanced up and down, peering into another cabinet from time to time. I offered him popcorn, doughnuts, and warm milk. "No," he said emphatically. "There is nothing here to satisfy."

That night as I lay in bed, fear overcame me. Was Swami telling me goodbye? Because if he was, I'd be out of business. If he was pulling the plug on me, where would I go? Swami, who knows everything about me and loves me anyway, has resisted trying to change me. My truculent nature he has left to circumstance and consciousness to correct. But when I told him that I feared losing him, he let me have it. A right jab to my fear and a left one to my doubt. I was KO'd by a skinny little guy in a sheet. Ouch. The mouse he gave to my consciousness required a steak to be placed over it.

"I will never leave you, Vicki, because you are in my heart and I am in yours. Never doubt that. Never." I looked at him with such longing that he almost wept. But he picked up the toaster and shook it, freeing it of crumbs and debris before wiping it down with a paper towel.

I went into the sunroom and sat down, wondering why I had never allowed myself to be fully loved by Swami until now. Death is the last enemy to be overcome and he was assuring me that even that would not separate us. We spiritual students are funny creatures, clinging and pushing away at the same time. We do not understand that everything is a mirror and that love itself

is indivisible. We are utterly, utterly safe, loved, and held. And some of us are fed by Swami—what a deal.

Larry's Turn

I ran into Larry last night and asked him point blank why he had skipped satsang. He sniffed and said that any satsang that would accept a grown man riding a stick pony was beneath him. "Larry, that joke is an old chestnut," I said, but Larry wasn't joking; he was sulking. I reported back to Swami what Larry had said about not being good enough for satsang. "He could learn a lot from Ruin," said Swami. "Just look at him. He has mastered the art of resting in the still point better than anyone else."

"That's it!" I said. "That's what's wrong with Larry. It's not that he's having a hard time accepting himself; he's jealous of Ruin. And so am I!" I threw my arms around Swami and wondered at his skills, not only as a guru, but as a therapist.

I called Larry the next morning and asked him to meet me at Dunkin' Donuts. Even though he brought Ruin along, I gave Larry my undivided attention. I usually let Ruin drink out of my coffee cup, but today I offered him nothing. Some things may not be apparent except to the trained observer, but Ruin has a thing or two to learn about hogging center stage. Today is Larry's turn and that is that.

Larry's jealousy of Ruin is persisting. I asked him why he couldn't let Ruin be what he was—a stick pony. "It's 'Ruin this and Ruin that,'" said Larry, obsessively. "Everybody loves Ruin and I am nothing without him."

"Well, Larry," I offered, "Nothing is the name of the game we're playing, after all." I thought this very wise of me. I looked around to see if anyone else was regarding me with new-found appreciation. All I saw was donut snarfing. Oh, well.

Larry stirred his coffee and took a bite out of his chocolate cake

donut. Ruin regarded him wisely. Undaunted by the jealousy, he sat there with his wisdom-eye wide open. (It was painted on.) Oh, to possess such aplomb in the midst of the cruel divisiveness of the mind. I wanted stick pony wisdom for my very own.

Sea Change

When Swami Z came into my consciousness, a sea change began to occur. We hear that life is but a dream and that we are only dreamed characters. How true. The paradoxical irony (if there is such a thing) is that the little Swami leads me directly to the Real. I am unable to do anything about it, but continue to write him. He does the rest. As Maharaji said, "God does everything."

Whatever we are doing in the kitchen is the right thing for us at the time. I never second-guess love. That would be tantamount to breaking an egg before it is laid. Swami is the chef and I am just his assistant. Yes, I did give him a place to stay, but he, being unreal, had to stay where I wrote him. As he says, "Stick with me. This is getting complicated."

Even Christ followed a predestined script. Gurdjieff taught that man cannot do, and with this I heartily agree. We are helpless puppets in the play of life. The saints and sages urge us to wake up, see the unreal and come to Reality. We are playthings of the divine, mere toys in the cosmic schoolroom. The lessons are about love.

> *"You live that you may learn to love.*
> *You love that you may learn to live.*
> *No other lesson is required of man."*
> Mikhail Naimy, The Book of Mirdad

So Swami Z is nothing but a figment of my imagination and when I let Vicki be in the script, I began to love her, too. In fact, that is the direct path to love for me. Loving the script and the characters. Swami has now wandered into the computer and is looking over my shoulder. I know that you are anxious to hear what he has to say.

"Come to satsang—the company of the wise." He could have ended it like that and elevated me to guru status. But no, he had to come back in and say, "In our case, the company of the weisenheimers." Darned killjoy. Ruin is the real guru anyway.

Summer with Swami Z

Swami is getting ready for a long, hot summer with the usual suspects. To that end, he has gone to the mall and bought us an inflatable swimming pool. It is not very big, but he suggests that we sit in a circle and put our feet in it while he speaks. Of course, this means that the talks will be outdoors and I will have to make the lemonade.

Larry is already here in hopes of getting the primo spot. According to him, Ruin is afraid of the water and will have to stay in the house. That takes all the fun out of satsang. Ruin carries the spirit of surrender and without that, we might as well be at a health fair. Rose and Jim are on the way and I am making the lemonade as fast as I can.

"Vicki," Swami says all of a sudden, "if you don't mind, I think you should stay in here and keep Ruin company." I looked at Swami and then at Ruin. Ruin was giving nothing away. If he was really afraid of the water, he was not going to admit it.

"But I don't want to," I whined. "Ruin can just get over his fear of the water. All he has to do is put his feet in." Now I saw the problem clearly. Ruin had no feet. How could I ask him to do something that was impossible? I felt a brief burst of compassion arise in my hard little heart.

"Okay," I said magnanimously, "Ruin and I will stay in the den and watch a movie." Swami patted me on the head and left the room. I looked over at Ruin and just had to add, "You do have eyes, don't you?" I was badly in need of satsang; no one needed it more than me. Ruin did not take the bait.

I looked closely at Ruin, propped against the couch cushion. I felt a mean streak arising that was not going away. So I gave in

to it. "Ruin," I said coldly, "would you like a popsicle?" Without waiting for him to reply, I went to the fridge and found a grape one. Taking off the paper, I held it in front of him. He didn't bat an eye.

I ate it slowly while I watched *Seabiscuit.* Even though Ruin got no popsicle that day, he remained the champ, just like in the movie. When the others came in from the backyard, all sweaty and with wet feet, I couldn't wait to hear what I had missed. But no one paid me the slightest bit of attention. It was all given to Ruin, the horse with no feet and no mouth to speak of. That's just not fair.

Swami hand-fed him tiny bits of butterscotch-chip cookies and Rose held a straw to his mouth while he sipped some strawberry milk. "Nuts," I thought to myself. "Nobody wants a whiner when a whinnier will do!" I was bested by a wooden stick with a stupid fuzzy head. Not only that, but he belonged to Larry. Larry and Ruin rode off into the distance about an hour later and Swami and I were left alone in the kitchen. Wearily, I glanced over at him. He arched his eyebrows and said that he wasn't pleased with my behavior.

Swami knew that I was jealous of Ruin and that is why he made me stay inside with him. I got to experience how isolating it is to be just a stick pony among men. But instead of compassion, I had felt nothing but petty negativity—a desire to come out on top. Ruin was too kind to ever let me know that, but Swami was not above taking me in hand. "I'm sorry," I said. "Next week I will stay in with him again."

"Yes," said Swami, "and I hope you have learned your lesson. Be kind to your stick-footed friends." This sounded a little stupid, but then I am the one making this up as I go along. Once I remembered that, I gave Swami a milk mustache and sent him to bed early. Ha!

Riding for a Fall

Although it is almost summer, Larry is riding for a fall. So help me Santa Claus, he rode into satsang today with a plastic raft around his waist and Ruin beneath him. Well, he has always been beneath Ruin, but that's another matter. Try and picture this—a geek on a stick with a ducky raft around his waist. Swami snickered until we all broke into helpless laughter. Rose blew milk through her nose. Of course, Larry didn't get it.

"What?" he said. "What is it with you guys? I'm taking Ruin in the pool and this ducky deal here will calm him down." He must have known this was a useless ploy. Ruin had already been parked kitchen counter-side and Larry was reaching for the plate of cookies. Swami said with a straight face, "Maybe it's time for Ruin to go in the pool with everybody else." Of course I couldn't help but chime in. "We just put our feet in the pool, remember?"

"Yes, Vicki, I am aware of that. But Ruin can just plant his little pole in there with the rest of you. It won't kill him."

"No," I snapped. "He's already dead. Just a stick, a toy, a thing!" Now the mob turned on me. Rose said with great and surprising venom, "Vicki, you of all people should know that Ruin is the real guru." Ruin had no reply. He was gazing sweetly at whatever stick ponies see.

"Well, if he's the real guru, why can't he wake us all up? Even Swami can't do that." Now it was Swami's turn to look pained. He just didn't look as serene as Ruin. "Can't wake you up, my hind foot!" he hollered. "You don't know the difference between bed rest and satsang. May as well be talking to a sack of sloths."

Larry continued to eat nonstop. He had lost the thread of the conversation three cookies back. Let it be said that Jim had been

149

quiet the whole time. Now it was his turn. "I think the lot of you are cuckoo," he said with a vehemence unknown to the gentle Jim. "Berserk, stark raving mad, nobody home at anyone's house. Me, I'm goin' in the pool." He took off his socks and shoes and stomped out the door, although quietly. If you think this escapade is gonna end by making sense, you haven't read enough Swami Z pieces. Come back next time and I will enlighten you about that.

Sitting Ducks

Outdoor satsang is terrific. Swami seems to be in his element. Of course, there is a picket fence around it and we are gathered around a vinyl swimming pool, but still—nature is close at hand. Yesterday we played under the sprinkler, which I remembered doing in my childhood. We ate cherry and banana popsicles and shrieked as the cool water hit our bare legs.

Swami's talk was definitely for the few, because there are only six of us, counting Swami himself. He kept bringing home the point that there is only the Self in all beings. The Self chitters down at us from a tree. The Self picks up the garbage. The Self wears polyester—and really shouldn't. I looked accusingly at Jim, but he is so sweetly unfashionable that it hurts. He was wearing a short-sleeved white dress shirt and a clip-on tie.

Larry was the Self with a mullet. Ruin was the Self elevated to cult status, at least in our small group. We were fatuous in our fondness for him. He gazed into the depths of our tiny vinyl pool as if he liked it. He didn't. Only Swami could have persuaded him to try it just this once. Now his little stick was wet at the bottom, but his inner look was imperturbable.

Knowing the Self is tricky; to be the Self that you know you are is even harder. In my case, the Self is a pig. I had my eye on the jumbo peanut butter cookies still warm from the oven. A fly briefly settled on one and I forgot that to swat him would be violating the principle of ahimsa. I waved my hand wildly over the cookies and Swami said, "Yes, Vicki, what is it?"

"There's a fly on one of the cookies," I said sharply.

"So!" he snapped back.

"I guess we better go ahead and eat them before they are contaminated," I said.

"Self-contamination, that's the problem," Swami said with surprising sweetness. "Only Vicki can stop contaminating Vicki." Larry couldn't contain his delight at my moment of reproof. "She does it to me all the time!" he said triumphantly.

"You can beat her at her own game," Swami said with a broad grin. "Pluck the fly off your own cookie." Not knowing what else to do, I yelled, "Food fight!" I began to hurl peanut butter cookies at Larry. He lobbed them back until Rose broke into tears. "Now you've gone and contaminated mine!" Turns out the Self in peanut butter cookies is on the endangered species list—at least in our backyard. Before I knew it, satsang was over and everyone was in a snit. Stay tuned for what goes on after dark....

Through the Eye of the Needle

Teaching the truth to the half-baked is no easy task. Just ask Swami Z. He has the unenviable job of putting people through the eye of the needle who just think they want to go. About half-way through, they change their minds, but by then it is too late. Kicking and screaming, waving pudgy arms in the air, they yell to Swami to save them. He does what he can, which is to butter them up a little so they go through more easily. At least that is how it appears to me. But what do I know; I am just a gizmo—a basting needle that helps Swami infuse people with the juiciness of surrender. Larry is a good case in point. As always, he rides Ruin to satsang, brings him in and often holds him on his lap. Once Swami fell so in love with Ruin that he forgot his point altogether. It was rather like samadhi-on-a-stick.

Larry is reluctant to let go of his attachments. In his Bible, a good mullet and a good stick pony beat a pair of aces every time. He is something of a gloater. He rides into Dunkin' Donuts, enters with Ruin and leaves with crumbs (and I exclude myself from that category). He thinks he is doing people a favor just by showing up. I disagree. I wouldn't be caught dead with Larry at a pig roast. We see each other at satsang, Dunkin' Donuts, and that's about it. Call me crazy, but Larry is a loser.

The Art of Being Nothing

Swami and I were sitting in the back yard. I asked him to tell me about patience. He said glibly, "Patience is the art of being nothing."

"It has to be more complicated than that," I said.

"Nope. Just be nothing and something will happen, but it won't be caused by you." I looked at this little guy sitting next to me—this one who occupies heart space and is one heck of a cookie maker—and I knew that he knew. The silence of the universe enveloped us. A bird flew by in blessing and a butterfly lit on a fading rose.

"There is no mental God," said Swami out of the clear blue. I looked up at him from across the swing. "There is no emotional God," he continued. "There is only the God of being and He belongs to the all." This went far beyond cookie-baking. Silence filled the space and we were just particles and waves. It was not deifying; it was idea-defying. Swami was thumbing his nose at religion, spiritual speculation, and human grandiosity. I could dig it.

Before Swami came to live with me, I was always looking for the truth. Now that he is ensconced in the kitchen, I have been able to let go of a good deal of my anxiety. His way is to get on with his life and this is a helpful thing for me. He is living out loud and letting me in on the truth of his being.

If he has arthritis, he yells. If he makes a good batch of cookies, he smiles ecstatically. If I frustrate him, he rolls his eyes. Of course, a lot of his tomfoolery is just that; but the essence of his being always seeps through. The mystery of Swami is that he doesn't exist. No matter how hard I try, I cannot bring him to

physical life. And yet he is a miracle-worker. He has changed my life for the better and has taught me how to beg for self-mercy until it hurts. And it often does.

Swami is against the parts of me that are out to do me harm and will not brook their presence for very long. It's not that he's psychic; more like what he says is in my best interests. When I get gloomy about my inability to overcome my mind, he steps up to the plate and acts it out for me so I don't have to. "Darned stinkin' thinkin'—I'd put out some mousetraps, but you'd catch your emotions in them and then where would we be?" Then we just end up sitting in silence and who can't profit from that?

So Much Love

*"Education is an admirable thing, but it is well to
remember from time to time that nothing that is worth
knowing can be taught."*

Oscar Wilde

Swami Z was sitting by the kitchen fire with a mug of hot cocoa
in his hands, warming them by the heat of the concoction. He
looked up at me and said, "So much love, so much love, what
is it for?" Now the Swami has never been much of one to
ask me questions, unless they are of the "What's for dinner?"
variety. Therefore, the question took me by surprise. I looked
at the skinny old thing in his ratty bathrobe, struck silent by his
love surplus. I would have taken him in my arms, but that had
proved dangerous on one occasion.

I had scooped him up in a dance of joy after eating one of his
sugar cookies and he had gone into a snit that lasted for days.
"Why do you think an old man like me comes to live with you—
to give, not to receive! Now put me down and wipe that grin
off your face." A large tear formed and ran quickly down my
face. I had no idea that it was there, so perilously close to my
idiocy. "There, you see," said Swami. "You need me—I don't
need you—except to give me a home."

Our home was modest, but it seemed to suit Swami well. Together
we had weathered quite a few storms—all caused by me,
apparently. The swami was an old tar, a seasoned veteran of the
briny emotional deeps. He returned to his intonation. "So much
love, so much love, what is it for?" I sat and picked at my cuticle
while pondering the question.

"Is it for me, Swami?"

He put his mug down carefully and looked so warmly at me that the answer arose in my heart, much like the steam rising from his mug. All I could do was nothing. Sometimes nothing is more than something—and that's the truth.

A Cocoa Mustache

Swami Z is very powerful; I have known that all along. Even though I kid about him, his is a seamless power that includes everything—from his socks to his little red knit hat. He has just come stomping in from the cold and is shivering in the kitchen.

"Hey, Swam," want some hot chocolate?"

"Sure do," he said, but only if you have marshmallows." I looked in the cabinets and found an opened bag fastened with a blue plastic clip. We were in business.

"Vicki," I think I know what you are supposed to be doing," he said imperiously.

I waited for the insult that was sure to follow. He drew his cup in front of him and begin stirring, watching the marshmallows melt.

"You are supposed to be doing exactly what you have been doing!"

"But, Swami," I said with a familiar whine. "I've been doing that all of my life, and look what kind of a life it is."

"Yeah, but it's yours," he said, taking a swig and emitting a pleasurable "ah."

"When your life changes without your trying to change it, that's real change."

I looked at him sitting there in all of his power, wearing a cocoa mustache. I knew that he was right. What could I do but nod my head.

At My Worst

"You're not a refrigerator and people aren't magnets."

Swami Z

The guru wants to see you at your worst. That is why Swami Z moved in with me—at least one of the reasons. The primary one is that my suffering opened the door for him and he seized the day. Before I knew it, he was taking birth on my iMac as if he owned the place. And now he is getting his own book. And he is still seeing me at my worst. Ack.

This morning I shoved him out of the way to do some cooking of my own. The recipe is for maple fudge. I haven't made it before, but it isn't rocket science. It does however, produce a sticky wicket situation. Put condensed milk, butter, white chocolate chips and nuts together and....

There are sticky spots all over the counter, on the can opener, in the sink, on my shirt and on the cabinet pulls. Swami is at the table pretending not to notice. He is also sulking about me claiming the right to the kitchen. I poured out the fudge into the foil-lined glass pan and begin to wipe up the stickiness. All he said was, "Way to go, Vicki. Way to go." I scowled and continued to wipe up all the spots I could see.

Larry knocked at the door and Swami answered. "Come in, come in, Larry. How's Ruin, how's my boy?" Ruin lifted his little nose, undoubtedly tempted by the maple smell emanating from the fudge. Larry pulled up a chair and I came over to Ruin with a small handful of walnuts. He looked at them and was having none of it, literally.

"Cut Ruin a piece of warm fudge, Vicki," Swami said. I was only too happy to oblige. I pulled the foil out of the pan and

inverted the fudge onto the cutting board. Ah, it was a beautiful sight to see. Perfect. I took a sharp knife and cut the first row of fudge. I carefully lifted out three pieces. The first one went to Ruin, the second to Swami and the third to Larry. I think that is a reasonable pecking order. I then returned to the counter and cut three pieces for myself. I think that is only right to reward the cook. Not that this is cutting edge spirituality, but satsang is not always about the words. This morning it was about music in our mouths.

Swami wiped Ruin's muzzle with a soapy rag and then he and Larry left. I thought Swami might have missed my wee spell of greed but he is incapable of fudging on me. "I hope you gain five pounds right around your middle," he said.

"I already have," I confessed. And tomorrow I'm making another recipe. "You're a recipe for disaster," he smirked. And, as I said, that is why he came to live with me.

Eden

"Let he who is without snit cast the first 'I told you so.'"

Swami Z

I wanted to ask Swami whether or not I had made any progress in self-escape. However, how was I to word such a question? I settled for putting it exactly like that. Swami sat down at the table and looked me straight in the eye. "Vicki," he said, "the answer escapes me. But I heard the question." He rose to put the kettle on and that gave me time to fall back and regroup.

When he sat back down, I tried to reformulate the question. "Have I," I faltered, "made the first step towards self-demolishment?" Silence. Then I heard someone knocking at the door. It was Larry. He had ridden over on Ruin just because he had nothing better to do. Satsang was not being held. We sat there together in a comfortable silence. Who cared whether I had escaped or remained a captive of my own thoughts. This was Eden.

Green with Envy

I have often wondered what Swami would say when I got so low that I felt like surrendering. Of course, no ego has ever been able to surrender; that is understood (but not by the ego). I asked him if there was any advice he had for me about maintaining spiritual practice when all is almost but not quite lost.

We sat at the table—me disconsolate and Swami a mere mirror for me. I gazed into his soul and saw the Self in all its silence. I loved the purity of his non-existence and prayed that he would one day become real. It was all I could do.

Whenever life bears down upon us, we must remember the concept of grace. It has something to do with God and nothing to do with us. Swami may be a fictitious cookie-maker, but he is also the love of my life. He transcends what I intend to say and voilà—I am changed into a different version of myself.

I am getting downright jealous of Ruin—that Teacher's Pet-on-a-Stick. Yesterday, Swami fed him cookie dough right from the bowl and then gently wiped his little mouth off. Who says that spiritual teachers don't have favorites? Swami knew that I was watching them out of the corner of my envy, so he made it excruciatingly obvious that he loved the little fake horse. I am not being a stick-in-the-mud, but the Swami-meister was slathering it on just so I could turn green with envy.

"Vicki thinks Ruin is just a silly old stick, but I love you, Ruin. You are the best stick pony in the whole wide world," said Swami.

"Bite me," was what I thought, but I recovered nicely (or so I thought). I asked Larry to stay for dinner. We were having fried hot dogs and he hates them.

A Turn for the Worse

Satsang was so much fun today. Swami had a light-heartedness about him that had little to do with circumstance. His arthritis has been bothering him, so I know that he isn't pain-free. He just seemed eternal as he sat there loving us all so deeply. Rose has changed markedly since satsangs began. She, who used to clutch her handbag so tightly that it was comical, has begun to show her inner beauty. The softness of Rose is showing through now as she listens to Swami speak.

"You people are not changing at all. Your suffering is at an all-time high. The dam may break and flood us all out of the house." We were surprised. Just when I thought progress was being made, Swami turns the car around and steers it in another direction altogether. That afternoon, things took a nasty turn. Rose had come down with a cold and was sniffling away at satsang, robbing it of purpose and meaning. At least that is what I thought. I kept it to myself, of course. Jim, Larry and Ruin just sat there expressionless. "If she blows that honker another time, I'm gonna blow," I thought.

Swami suddenly broke off in the middle of a sentence (I wasn't listening to him, but to myself). "Vicki, would you like to tell the class what you were just thinking? I know that you were close to God just now." He looked positively menacing.

"I, uh, I uh...." The words were stuck in a glob of guilt and I couldn't get them out. To make it worse, Rose sneezed and I said, "God bless you." And He did, apparently. Swami resumed what he was saying and I was temporarily off the hook. But I had better examine the effects I was having on myself. If all I could be honest about was how irritated I was with Rose's cold, how could I ever come to the living truth?

Larry was the only one who seemed unmoved. He is about 60% automaton and 40% human. The latter is thanks to Ruin, who sits beside him gazing into eternity. "What do you think the problem is, Swami?" Larry asked. "Because some of us are willing to change." Ha! I couldn't wait to hear what Swami said next. Instead of speaking, he sat motionless for at least a full minute. Then he said, very sharply, "Then change now!"

Jim jumped and I sat up straighter. Larry knocked Ruin onto the floor altogether and said defensively, "Okay. Okie dokie. I'm changing. Now." We gazed at him collectively until he turned bright red.

Larry said unexpectedly, "I have something to admit. No one loves me." You could have heard a pin drop. You could have heard the world turn. No one wanted to say that, so Larry had said it for them. Swami slumped slightly. Then he said, so gently that a tear fell from my eye, "Vicki loves you."

What? Me? Love Larry? I couldn't lie because I had just said that honesty joins me to God. What in the heck is going to join me to Larry? I didn't love him—couldn't love him. Swami was driving the satsang-mobile at 90 miles an hour and I wanted to get out.

"Hmmmpph!" said Jim, uncharacteristically bold. "I love Larry a lot more than Vicki does. I love him more than, more than...." He slowly trailed off. Swami looked at me and let me off the hook. "Vicki loves Larry, too, Jim. She just doesn't know how to get in touch with her feelings." Swami was on thin ice with me and he knew it.

Rose saved the day for all of us. She reached into her pocketbook and took out a small digital camera. She took a picture of satsang right in the middle of it changing. I must say that it was a beautiful sight. She caught Swami's charisma, Jim's idealism,

Larry's stupidity, and my enormous appetite for living on the edge, all in one small click. Oh, yes, Ruin's mane had never looked so handsome. Satsang over.

In a Rut

I was worn out from housecleaning and was also in a rut. Satsang had fallen into a routine and I found myself guessing what Swami would say next. I was taking him for granted. The usual suspects were there. Swami was holding forth and I was just about to nod off. Suddenly Rose shot her hand up. "Yes, Rose, what is it?" asked Swami.

"I want to know if you think any of us are going to be enlightened any time soon—or is this just a big waste of time for you?" Rose could've been reading my mind.

"Rose, we are not here to make progress. We are here to make you disappear. And that takes time." Rose looked dissatisfied with that answer. I understood where she was coming from.

"What will happen when we disappear?" I ventured to ask. Swami always applied more pressure to me than he did to the others. "I, for one, will be very glad," he said with mock disgust. At least I hoped it was mock.

Larry giggled. "I think that when Vicki disappears, we won't have any place to meet."

Glad that I had a reason to be, I asked Swami to get to the bottom line. "Will we know love when we have disappeared?"

"That is all you will know," replied Swami. "And all that you will need to know." Rose wiped her eyes, Jim gave a sigh, and Larry, well, Larry— he just gave Ruin a little pat.

A Measly Excuse

Larry knocked on the door, barged in and sat right down beside me at the kitchen table. "Ruin is sick," he said with a serious look. "He has the measles."

"Oh, that's ridiculous," I barked. "Stick ponies don't get sick. Wake up." I picked Ruin up and looked him over. "Measles my hind leg; he's got Hawaiian Punch all over him."

Swami handed me the dish rag and I healed him right on the spot. Call me crazy, but I suddenly felt better. Silliness is next to Larry and I am next to Swami and all's right with the world.

Snit City

I have a lot of snits. I am not saying that snits are a good thing; I'm just owning up to what goes on in my antebellum cerebellum good-for-nothing brain. "Vicki, if you have one more snit today, you are over the legal limit. Now zip it," Swami snapped.

I knew that he was right. Often I snitted on people unconsciously and felt indignant when I got one in return. It's rather like forgetting you ordered a red wool hat and then on the hottest day of the year, there it is. You ordered it; you just forgot. Swami sings off-key when I have a snit that he isn't up to dealing with. "I'll be seeing you in all the old familiar places that this heart of mine embraces...." And I am just snitting away to my heart's content.

If you have ever had a good cleansing snit, you know that others have them, too. They just have them when you're not looking. Only spiritual masters are above snitting. Swami has teaching snits, which don't really count. He fakes anger so that we will take our lessons more seriously. At least that is what I tell myself. Occasionally, I see the truth of what is really going on and I "schmoo over" with love for him. And one good schmoo wipes out ten snits—at least that is what I have been told.

This morning I wearily dragged myself around the kitchen. Depression has hit and even Swami cannot take it away. He is not a magician, but a magi and there is a difference. He continues to give satsang and I attend; but my heart is suddenly not in it. Perhaps I need a good colonic.

Larry drops by. He props Ruin in the corner and grabs a chair. Swami pours him tea and serves him warm sugar cookies. He is one lucky dude, if you ask me. "Vicki," says Larry, "have you ever thought that you are in spiritual overdose? That maybe

you need to go on an anti-spiritual retreat. A little boot-scootin' boogie kind of trip?"

He had a point. I had not left Swami's side for many moons. Not only that, I had no desire to be out of his sight. I was committed to him, depressed as I had become. Satsang reflected my weariness that day. "Swami," asked Jim, "if God is here and now, why aren't we any different?"

"Because you are not here and now. You are now and then." Swami sighed. Ruin stirred briefly. Rose had knocked him over. She softly re-propped him, patting his soft brown head. He was a magi, too—born in a stable. Swami spoke words that my brain filtered down to my heart. Stuff like I had heard so many times before. "Your depression is grief. What are you missing? Who are you missing?" I was dozing off. Suddenly Swami shot up out of his chair and left the room....

Quickening

What we seek is quickening—the spiritual intuition that cuts through the mental machinery and zaps it. Swami swept into the room like a burst of spring blossoms. Freshness wafted into our collective hearts, for this was Swami come to enlighten us. We all sat up straighter. Something told me that this was for keeps. "I have cut the ties that bind you," he said.

Larry looked panic-stricken. "Are you talking about cable, because I wanna watch something tonight."

"No, Larry, I am talking about what keeps you tied to yourself like a hitching post—like you tie Ruin to the parking meter." Rose and Jim clearly had no better guess than Larry. What was it about Swami that was different? He hadn't gotten his ears lowered—that wasn't it. He hadn't had a facial or gotten a new shirt. I knew what it was. He had bought a new cookie shooter. No, that wasn't right, either.

Swami sat in his chair surveying the stupidity of his students. "I have ended your ignorance once and for all. Don't you feel clear-headed and suddenly sane?" There were no takers. Not a single one of us managed to wake up even one tiny bit more. Surely, enlightenment can be given away if the owner has more than enough to share?

I pondered this question as we dully filed into the kitchen for pumpkin cupcakes. Swami looked buoyantly undisturbed by it all. Last night he had been morose—and now this. Something was up and it wasn't the time on Ruin's parking meter. Swami spoke, albeit with whipped cream on his chin. "I have decided that all of you are lacking the seventh sense," he said.

My ears perked up as high as Ruin's. What was he talking

about? "The sixth sense is psi," he said. "The seventh sense is a sense of humor. I am not sure that any of you people have one." The phrase, "you people," always meant trouble. We had become one giant annoyance to Swami. Our snitting had reached an intolerable level and he was just about to kick us out of the nest. Squawk.

"Enlightenment should be fun. It should elate you; if nothing else it should elevate you," he went on. "Vicki has a pretty good sense of humor when she writes about me. But when she leaves the computer, she forgets how funny being human is. She mopes around with the best of them." I was annoyed. I looked around. Rose was looking dour. Jim was stiff as a soldier and Larry was teed off. Ruin looked the other way. I couldn't expect him to have a sense of humor. He was just a stick horse. "All of you are sitting there looking insulted!" said Swami Z.

"No snit, Swami," said Larry from the back row. Suddenly Rose giggled. That let the rest of us off the hook and we began to relax. Satsang ended with Swami doing an impromptu soft shoe and the rest of us singing with our mouths full.

Not Fade Away

Sometimes Vicki forgot to pay attention to Swami and he would begin to fade away before her very eyes. Swamis are like that. He was always there in such an integral way. She couldn't imagine his absence. There had been times when he had gone away, but he had always returned. That seemed to be a part of his teaching, for Vicki believed in departures.

He sat at the table sipping tea and looking into space. Dust motes danced in the shaft of light coming in through the window. I saw them turn and make a beeline toward Swami. None came in my direction. How odd is that?

"You old coot!" I exclaimed. "You're a mote magnet. How can you do that?"

Swami squinted at the motes moving visibly toward him in the cone of light. As he watched, I watched him—begin to fade away. Yes—his shirt and pants were still there, but there was only light where Swami used to be. Could that light speak? I yelled into the light. "Swami, where are you?" He rearranged himself as skin and bones and voice. "I'm right here where I've always been. Nowhere in particular."

I sensed a change in our relationship, for how can matter speak to spirit and be heard? Did it matter? Had I been heard? What's up with that? Swami reached across the table and took my hand. He planted a kiss upon my palm and asked me to pass the cream. Had I passed the test—and if so, what was it?

Nirvana

When Swami came into the kitchen from his nap, I told him I had a question to ask him about how he became invisible. "Oh, that," he said, "that's not worth asking about. Ask me something with some meat in it—like why I don't make pretzels or Rice Krispie Treats—or dog biscuits."

"Okay, I'll ask. Why don't you make anything besides cookies?"

"Because that is what you expect me to make. And you expect me to enlighten you and so I do."

"I sure as heck don't feel enlightened," I whined. About that time the oven timer went off and I was saved for the moment, but I wasn't about to let this subject die away.

"I also expect you to disappear right in front of my eyes and never return."

"If you expect what you get, you will never be disappointed." And with that, Swami turned on his heel and disappeared yet again.

For what it's worth, Swami can be a pain in the old patootie. He has the annoying habit of praising everyone in satsang but me. Rose came in smelling like Charlie the Tuna and Swami kissed her and said she smelled like heaven. Jim's turn came when he told Swami that he had been working on breathing consciously. "Fine, Jim. Great! You're going to end up teaching us all a thing or two."

I scowled. When was the last time that Swami made me a good example. My brow furrowed up like Edward R. Murrow. Dang! I had to do something to get attention. So I made up a question and raised my hand. "Yes, Vicki," said Swami.

"Can you explain nirvana—do you experience it on a regular basis?"

"Only if I remember to eat my bran," he said. Okay, he was clearly not taken in by my ruse. So I sat there in complete silence for the rest of satsang. I could have been a stone. As Swami walked by, he patted me on the head and said, "Well done." Apparently my silence, which reeked as badly as Rose's tuna, earned more for me than any stupid question I could raise.

Spiritual Honesty

Spiritual honesty is a sometimes thing. Often we are too immersed in ego to hear the voice of truth, although it is always trying to break through the charade of being separate from anyone or anything. Usually we are brought home to honesty by a certain amount of pain or suffering. The moment we are forced to witness the pain, we return to honesty. I imagine someone or something in heaven rejoices even a small bit when this happens.

I write the characters of Swami Z and friends without allowing myself to think about them. I just turn my head in their direction and there they are, full-blown in their honesty and idiocy for all the world to see. There is something about a loser on a stick pony that frees everyone up to relax a little bit and stop taking their spirituality so seriously. At least I hope so.

Swami says that he moved into Vicki's kitchen because she opened the door through her suffering, or something to that effect. He never tried to take it away; he only began his guru shenanigans right there in front of God and everybody. I mean, who could believe that a cookie-making, grizzled old son-of-a-gun could know a thing about advaita vedanta or heaven forbid, how to teach a bunch of miscreants about the secret of life. So far he hasn't.

But the small but stubborn crew are heavily invested in attending satsang; on most days we can call that a wasted effort, but every now and then something will sprout that isn't coming from Ruin's feedbag. A real sprig of truth will turn up in someone's brain. Take last night....

I won't bore you with the details, but a certain devotee named Larry was heard to say this, "I know what will set me free." We all turned and looked at him with great disdain. I even snorted.

"No, I don't mean what will enlighten me," he said, "I mean what will set me free." Turns out Swami had tied his shoelaces together while we were all meditating and he was just about to untie the knots. Such a satsang, such a teacher—and soon we would all be having a party in our mouth. The oven timer just went off, meaning that even if satsang wasn't over, it might as well have been.

A Disciple of a Concept

This morning Swami was giving me a private lesson. "Why do you always want more of 'enough'? Enough is enough. Stupid students always want to put a head on top of their head and trust me, one of your heads is enough. I don't want more. But you— sheesh!"

He was brandishing a hot, greasy spatula as he spoke. It was 10:00 a.m. and the cookies were piling up on a large plate. Today it was snickerdoodles and I could almost hear them laughing at me. Nevertheless, I ate several while listening to his rant.

"I didn't say anything about wanting more than enough," I said weakly, wiping the crumbs from my lap.

"Oh, you don't have to," he snorted. "You take more cookies than you need. Not just you. Everybody. Do you think these cookies make themselves? No, I feed people because it's what I do. It's who I am. But you people, you make it difficult for me to get my message out there."

I was totally flummoxed. Where did this tirade come from? We had been eating his cookies for years and he knew all about us. He knew our weaknesses and sins like nobody else. What was eating him?

He didn't sit so much as throw himself down on the couch in the sunroom. "Look, Vicki, the sun is shining enough. The grass is growing enough. Enough is enough!"

I didn't know what to say. His logic and his argument had blasted out of nowhere for no reason. "Sure," I said. "I'm as dumb as a rock; I guess I forgot I was a greedy rock. A big, fat, dumb, greedy rock."

Uh, oh. Another tirade was beginning. "Why is it you are always putting yourself down? Big, fat, dumb rocks are not why I am here. I am here to feed people who are hungry. But enough is enough. Now I have work to do."

I got the message. I always did. I guess that is why he came to live with me. I understood just enough for him to keep feeding me. Maybe one day enough will be enough. It isn't easy living with a little imaginary swami, trust me. You certainly can't trust him. Just this morning I stumbled into the kitchen to find Swami busily at work with a broom and dust pan. I hadn't even had tea yet and if I asked him what he was doing, it would open a can of worms that wouldn't go well with tea. With a big sigh, he continued to sweep things into the dust pan. Feigning fatigue, he plopped down at the table and said nothing.

Of course, I bit. I always do. "So what's up with the sweeping, Swami?"

"Just cleaning up all of the adjectives that keep piling up around here," he said. "All of the impossible statements and huffy attitudes that seem to breed around this place."

I waited for him to continue. I got up and put the kettle on and sat back down. Sure enough, he couldn't keep it to himself. "Some of these adjectives are clogging up my sinuses," he said, reaching into the pocket of his ratty old robe to withdraw a giant handkerchief. He blew his nose noisily.

"Well, it looks like you did a fine job of sweeping them up," I said, hoping that humoring him was the way to avoid further conversation. He rose and walked across the room to get the old fly swatter from its hook on the wall. He actually swatted something on the window sill, saying, "Darned concepts!"

I knew what he meant. He is the "I am" concept itself. I didn't want to tell him I had made him up and was now paying the

price. I just went over and gave him a hug. He is the teacher, after all. That makes me a disciple of a concept. Gotta love it.

When There is Nothing Left to Do, Do It!

I bumped into Swami as he came in from the grocery with a few bags of baking ingredients. Butter, sugar, flour, cinnamon, vanilla—ecstasy. No, the ecstasy would come as we ate the cookies. I was flying around wiping down the counters and mumbling to myself about how he messed up the kitchen on a daily basis.

"Sit down and take a load off," he said, which was disconcerting because he himself had a load of supplies.

So I sat down and pulled the plate of yesterday's cookies towards me. He put the groceries away while I watched him work. Such a wiry little guy; if he weren't so senile, it would be impressive. Oh, yes, he's losing quite a bit of his mind. The old gray matter, she ain't what she used to be....

Reading my mind, he whirled around and gave kitchen satsang to a crowd of one—me! It went like this.

"When there is nothing to say, don't say it. When there is nothing to do, don't do it. On the other hand," he said, looking down at his hands, "I need to wash mine." And with that he turned around and faced the kitchen sink. In that satsang, I got everything AND the kitchen sink. Want a cookie?

A Question

"The fool doth think he is wise, but the wise man
knows himself to be a fool."

William Shakespeare

I had a question forming in the back of my mind. Actually it had been slowly growing there for years and I thought that I knew the answer. Although the question could not be put entirely into words, I will try to give the gist of it. Will there ever be an end to this longing for love, this fear of losing love, this hope of winning love as yet unseen?

"Shush," said Swami. "I get it. I get it. You're hoping that I can tell you something that you wouldn't hear if I shouted from the rooftops." He looked as pathetic as ever. I wanted to rush over and embrace him, so shaky was his stance, so fragile was his old body. I knew that eventually his brain cells would begin to die from sheer age. What a loss—and yet I knew that I would always remember him and long for his love. I was thinking of the day when he would no longer be on this earth with me. And, of course, he had other disciples who would miss him, too.

"Let me tell you something that may surprise you," said Swami Z, deftly flipping a cobweb from the corner with his spatula. "When you can contain the whole world inside your heart, they will never forget you—impossible. They will be unable to not love you. You will not have to beg for the leavings of love. You will have the recipe for love itself."

"But what about me loving them?" That was my question as well. I long to keep loving some people who are not interested in returning my love.

"What do you care?" he said. Patiently, he repeated, "When you can keep them in your heart, you will never again have to leave home to find love. It will find you. Just like you found me." And then he added, "You didn't hear a word I said." Maybe someday.

On the Brink

Swami thinks that I am on the brink of being established in the Self. He also thinks that cutting butter into enlightenment makes it taste better. Go figure. I have to take him with a grain of salt, and salt is not good for my blood pressure; but then, neither is he. Witness the following conversation.

"Good morning, Vicki. I think you are very, very close to getting it." He stares at me fixedly, as if to cement me into his visual scrapbook. But then he comes closer and I see that he is removing a hair from my shirt.

"I think that once I get it, I will probably misplace it," I said. "I can't find the egg timer anywhere. I turned the kitchen upside down yesterday looking for it."

"Your mind is like a junk drawer," he said, using a familiar theme. "You have all of these odd little bits and pieces of unnecessary stuff crammed into a very small space." He emphasized the word "very."

We sat drinking our tea once I had poured us up two stiff mugs of it. I took mine with creamer, whereas Swami didn't. He seemed to be bent on pursuing the theme of me getting affixed on the Self like a postage stamp. "You've got it all wrong about being established in the Self. Vicki doesn't get established in it; she goes away for good." I hate to say it, but he beamed radiantly at the very thought of my disappearance.

I had always looked forward to being established in the Self; now it appeared that I would have to disappear. Who knows, I might be the last cookie on Swami's plate. He was getting a little long in the tooth. He had been living with me for over ten years now.

I took a moment to savor the flavor of this vanilla-scented little man. I almost felt kindly towards him, but then he broke the spell. "Vicki," he said crisply, "when you disappear, can I have your copper pots?"

"Copper, schmopper," I mumbled, "whatever...." And another day at Chez Cookie Crumbles began. I told Swami that I was writing about him online. He did a little jig. "Hot diggity," he said, and then again, "Hot diggity. Now maybe you will get off my back for just a little bit."

Truth to tell, he is never happier than when people are talking about him. He may make noises about being enlightened, but he makes even more when he gets wind that people are listening to what he has to say. He doesn't seem to mind that he is a bit of fiction, but then so are we all.

I can dress him up to look like Lady Gaga and there is not a darned thing he can do about it. I can make him sing falsetto or play the ukulele. Even though he is enlightened, he has to let his karma play out. I am so into exposing him for what he is all about.

Food Fight

I decided to ask Swami a question: "Why does my life always seem so screwed up?"

He was wearing his ratty old bathrobe and the few hairs on his head stood straight up. He not only gave me static; it styled his hair. I knew if I touched him, I would get a shock, so I restrained myself.

His look was dyspeptic, his reply was dysfunctional, and yet he was my guru. Nah, probably not. If he was my guru, he could have cleared a place in the vast wasteland of my mind. He hadn't even managed to bush-hog an acre of it yet.

This is what he said: "Your life doesn't seem screwed up; it actually is screwed up."

I choked on my bran muffin, which was as dry as his wit. I gazed into his rheumy eyes. He gazed back. Then he slapped me on the back, presumably to stop my choking.

I slapped back. A fight ensued. A food fight. I threw the muffin at him and he poured his cocoa on my head. If living with a grizzled old guru has made me crazy, imagine what I would be without him. If you say worse off, that will throw me into a tizzy and enough things have been thrown today already.

Biting The Big Twinkie

Satsang was interesting tonight, to say the least. Death was on the agenda and Swami wasn't going to let us off the hook. "One day you will all be food for worms," he said with mock ferociousness. Almost as if he enjoyed the concept.

"Death is not for sissies," he went on. "Be a good idea for some of you to die before you die. Bite the Big Twinkie. Do the Dirt Dance."

Larry's hand shot up. "Swami, I live in a trailer park and ride a stick pony. I'm already living on the edge. But I ain't ready to die."

Swami was relentless. "I am looking forward to your death because then I will have Ruin all to myself."

That hit a nerve. A huge nerve. We all snickered and looked at Ruin propped against Larry's chair. We all thought Larry would ride Ruin into the hereafter since they were joined at the hip. Ruin said nothing. Apparently it "made no never mind" to him.

"Ruin is the embodiment of wisdom, as we all know. And wisdom is who we are."

Larry had no finer sensibilities; there was no shred of discretion in his DNA. "That settles it then. I am not dying because I will never be separated from Ruin."

Swami said heartlessly, "Ruin is a stick pony. He's a dead thing already."

But this satsang on death simply would not, to use an expression, stick. Something in us knew the living truth and as soon as Swami shut up, we were going to feed it blueberry muffins.

And So to Bed

"I asked the river
About its destination
And came out lucky:
It babbled about nothing
And never came to a point."

Gyosen

Swami has been cranky lately. Snapping at Larry to quit overfeeding Ruin. Telling me to get a life. Yes, that's what he said to me just yesterday. I was telling him that he needed to cut back on his salt and he groused, "Vicki, get a life!"

I looked at him. Through the years he had grown a wee bit rotund. Given, he was a small man, but I was worried about his pot belly. He looked like an elf that could easily get stuck in a Keebler's tree. Not only that, but he had grown a bit hard of hearing. He was mistaking Larry's shave and a haircut knock for our next-door neighbor's. I caught him putting gravy on his cake and that just isn't right.

He can still read minds, though. As I was typing this, he barked at me, "Gravy is good on cake. Try it one of these days." Maybe he is journeying from the cradle to the gravy and is not senile at all.

I have my own set of problems. I have less and less patience with fools like Larry. Oh, I know he is just another projection on the movie screen of the Self, but I am ready to go to the refreshment stand. I have given up on enlightenment and am satisfied that being a dim bulb is all I can manage.

Some things have gotten better. We jump in the deep end of silence easily and float blissfully together. We sit on the swing

in the backyard and look up at the shifting clouds. We walk to the park and witness the miracle of children playing and dogs romping.

I guess you might say that Swami and I indulge in the play of consciousness. We are blessed to have our little satsang gang to hang out with. There is an endless plate of cookies and of foolish questions that deserve no answer.

Well, it's time to pull the curtains on another day with Swami. He has pulled the rug out from under me a million times—the least I can do is pull the curtains gracefully. And so to bed.

The Last Waltz

*"Rest as the ocean itself
And you will never sink again."*
Arjuna Nick Ardagh

Swami and I have been dancing together for a long time now. Where once I thought he had two left feet, now I know he is the One.

Sometimes he sweeps me off my feet and whirls me around the cosmos, emptying my pockets of all grains of sorrow.

Who is Swami Z and why did he come to live with me?

My heart was breaking when I first opened the door and let him in. It soon became clear that he knew all about me, wanted to heal me. But I didn't take him seriously.

We sat at the kitchen table for long hours, him looking into my very soul, doing nothing but being obedient to my script. He played his role beautifully. Like all human beings, I had him confused with doing. I thought he was about making me laugh, about making me cookies. I forgot that he was a made-up dude.

I began sharing him with online readers. At one point I actually materialized him. I was out walking one evening and met a man who was visiting his son from India. We introduced ourselves. He was elderly and very tiny. I engaged him in conversation and we walked together. I told him my husband was dying and I was so tired and wounded.

He said that he was a Hindu and I could tell he had a deep and abiding faith. "I am now an old man," he said. "I like to give people what they want. Is there anything you would like to ask of me?"

"I would like to know peace," I said.

"Yes, Vicki," he said, actually using my name like I have Swami Z do. "I will pray for your peace."

I told a few friends laughingly that I had materialized Swami Z. And I have come to a deep inner peace. So who can say who is doing what to whom and how anything can be managed outside of one's very own Self. I bow to all teachers everywhere who now reside in the One Heart.

I hope you know that Swami Z, although a piece of fiction, has leapt off the printed page and is running amok goodness knows where. Reminds me of the Beatles Song, "Across the Universe." Look for him everywhere.

"There is nothing to add to what is true and final. Likewise, there is nothing to subtract. But the mind would be ever 'doing.' Let it do what it likes. It ain't you."

The silence that follows the reading of this last page is who you are. I have relied on my own Self to bring these stories to the light. May they be received with open hearts and passed along when you are done with them. Swami would want it that way.

ABOUT THE AUTHOR

Vicki Woodyard received a B.S. degree, *magna cum laude*, in English and Psychology from the University of Memphis. She was born in Memphis, Tennessee, and makes her home in Atlanta. She has spent her life on the spiritual path. Vicki's first book is *Life With A Hole In It: That's How The Light Gets In.*

Her website is www.vickiwoodyard.com

"This is good reading. It made me smile and laugh. The words are drenched with love and a sense of humor along with reverence and awe for the mystery of life. I recommend this book!"

Scott Kiloby, author of *Reflections of the One Life*, *Love's Quiet Revolution*, **and** *Living Realization*

"Your words, always heart-driven, are able to rattle the bars on the mind-cage we all live in."

Elsa Bailey, Concord, CA

"A close-to-the-bone book about love, death, loss, and...love. Heartbreakingly honest, brave and inspiring."

Greg Goode, Author of *Standing as Awareness* **and** *Direct Path: A User Guide*

"Very readable, life-affirming and filled with deep compassion. Highly recommended."

Chuck Hillig, Author of *Enlightenment for Beginners*, *Seeds for the Soul*, *Looking for God: Seeing the Whole in One*, *The Way IT Is*, **and** *The Magic King*

Praise for *Life With A Hole In It: That's How The Light Gets In*

"This is a book of truth, wisdom and humor. It comes from the bones, not the brain. A magnificent brew. Buy this book!"

Mary Margaret Moore, author of *I Come As A Brother: The Teachings of Bartholomew*

"Vicki is one of those rare souls who can show us all how to turn the charcoal into a diamond through her creativity. Her words can guide us all to a place of healing."

Bernie Siegel, MD, author of *Faith, Hope & Healing* and *365 Prescriptions For The Soul*

"Vicki's unique voice is honest, direct, spiritually raw."

Josh Baran, author of *The Tao of Now*

"Vicki Woodyard is one of the treasures of spiritual literature."

Jerry Katz, Nonduality.com, Editor: *One-Essential Writings on Nonduality*

"Your words are working; I can feel them in my bones."

Reader Comment

"Ablaze with light!"

Ronda La Rue, author of *Remembering Who You Really Are* and *The Art of Living Your Destiny!*

Also by Vicki Woodyard

Life With A Hole In It: That's How The Light Gets In

www.vickiwoodyard.com